The Authority of a Bishop

The Authority of a Bishop

John Halliburton

First published in Great Britain 1987
SPCK
Holy Trinity Church
Marylebone Road
London NW1 4DU

British Library Cataloguing in Publication Data

Halliburton, John
     The authority of a bishop.
     1. Church of England——Bishops
     I. Title
     262'.12   BX5176

     ISBN 0–281–04224–1

Printed in Great Britain by Hollen Street Press Ltd, Slough

Contents

Preface

Nine years as a member of the Church of England Doctrine Commission and twelve as a consultant to the Anglican–Roman Catholic International Commission have left me a sadder and (I hope) a wiser man. Sadder, because through the meetings of the Doctrine Commission I have begun to see some of the difficulties and frustrations that bishops of the Church of England face when controversy over Christian doctrine is given wide publicity. In so many ways they are being asked to assume a traditional role as 'guardians of the faith' and upholders of 'what we all believe'. They are at the same time hemmed in by so many restraints, the General Synod, Parliament and the persuasive attraction of 'theologians at large'. Together they may reach a common mind; but their voice is often muffled by a web of bureaucracy and establishment shot through with the bright colours of other people's theological sophistication. I sympathize. They deserve a greater freedom and I hope I have done a little here to point a way.

My years with the Anglican Roman Catholic International Commission have left me wiser in the sense that I believe that our brothers and sisters in the Roman Catholic Church regard us with particular affection. They believe, they say, that we in the Anglican Communion have retained in part 'Catholic traditions and structure'. They value the fact that we are an episcopal communion and are anxious that we should behave as such.

Among many other duties, all bishops are called to the 'ministry of discernment', to lead their people in the endless quest for Christian truth, to speak for them and to them and to bear the brunt when there is much heat and little light. When we are on the brink of reunion with the Roman Church, it will be our bishops, not just our theologians, who will lead us into the exploration of the potential of life in partnership with another and vaster communion of churches. It is they who will speak for the Anglican Communion, they who will voice our fears, they who will carry with them the convictions of all who see in a united Church a greater hope for the human race. For this once more they require a greater freedom, a greater confidence in their office.

This book is dedicated to them, but not written for them. They are all too familiar with most of the issues that I have raised. We on the other hand, the clergy and people of the Christian Church, must learn to appreciate something of the burden that is laid upon our bishops. They are not distant figures. Like the Good Shepherd they want to know us and be known of us, for it is us whom they credit with and value for communicating to them what we have learned in our simplest attempts at Christian discipleship. If we trust our bishop to speak for us, we have no need to restrain him by majority vote in a forum of our own devising. If he speaks, this does not mean that he will not listen again. He knows very well that we are partners with him in a common exploration and that the truth and unity of the Church of the future will be the achievement of us all.

I am most grateful to the Bishop of London for his kindness in reading the typescript with such care and for some helpful suggestions and important corrections which I have done my best to incorporate in the final revision. I am grateful also to the Bishop of Chichester for drawing my attention to the need for a discussion of the ordination of women to the priesthood in the context of a book on episcopal authority. The second excursus was written entirely at his suggestion.

I am sorry not to have been able to refer more frequently to an important study of a closely related theme which appeared shortly after my revised typescript had been sent to the publishers. *The Synod of Westminster: Do We Need It?* (edited by Peter Moore) includes some excellent studies of issues I have dealt with all too inadequately in my own book, and has the advantage of having been written by authors the majority of whom have first-hand experience of synodical government in the Church of England today. I hope very much, therefore, that Peter Moore's collection of essays will always be close at hand when readers are struggling with *The Authority of a Bishop*; but that at the same time the theological perspectives of this book may illuminate some of the issues to which the contributors to *The Synod of Westminster* have rightly and urgently drawn our attention.

March 1986   JOHN HALLIBURTON

1 Introduction – Decision-making in a Divided Church

In a cathedral church, one First Sunday after Christmas, the preacher was explaining that the Gospel accounts of the virgin birth had no foundation in history. Joseph was Jesus' real father, Mary was not a virgin when she conceived and the evangelists had written up the story of virginal conception on the basis of certain Old Testament texts in order to strengthen Christian belief in Jesus as Messiah and Son of God. The atmosphere in the cathedral was electric with hostility. Even the verger had deserted his chair by the control panel to the amplification system and was pacing the south transept. Without a word being said, it was quite clear that so far as the congregation was concerned, the preacher was wrong and they were right. A whole season of Christmas hymns and carol services had told them that God for our salvation became man in the womb of the Virgin Mary. That is what everyone believed. Why should this extraordinary clergyman tell them otherwise?

They were not to know at the time that this challenge to the traditional belief of the Church of England was to reach national proportions and to be given widespread publicity by the media. Reactions to such challenges in recent years have shown that the Church of England, by and large, does not take kindly to a theological 'rocking of the boat'. History has shown it to be a remarkably conservative body which has responded in anger and indignation to the presentation of new insights, from the views of those who supported Charles Darwin in the nineteenth century to the public utterances of liberal theologians of our own day. Despite the fact that the Church to its credit has very often absorbed these new insights and produced a richer and more contemporary theology, the mounting of an offensive in letters to the press and to church leaders has always seemed an inevitable preliminary to any serious theological reconsideration. The cry goes up, 'Someone is denying our faith. Why doesn't somebody do something?' But the question remains, Who is to 'do something' and what are they to do?

Some in the Church of England may look with envy at the Roman Catholic Communion where the whole process of decision-making and the 'definition' of doctrine seems much more straight-forward. Roman Catholics are largely aware that decisions in matters of faith and morals lie ultimately with the bishops in communion with the see of Rome. In these days they are glad to know that full consultation with representatives of the Church, clerical and lay, European and non-European, is no mere formality. The event of the Second Vatican Council is sufficient to show that a powerful groundswell of new thinking and the claims of hitherto poorly-represented cultures have led to the profound renewal and reform heralded by the conciliar documents. But in the last resort, Roman Catholics know that when a decision has to be made, it happens at Rome and it carries with it the authority of the bishops in council, and that of the Bishop of Rome in particular, who in virtue of his office, speaks in the name of the whole Church. Such a system has its drawbacks of course: clergy and laity alike suffer from what in its worst manifestations seems a Procrustean bed and an offence to human liberty. Many an Anglican is glad for that reason alone not to be a Roman Catholic. But at least in the Roman Church decisions are made and boundaries drawn, which makes some anxious for this kind of security in the Church of England.

But where is authority located in the Church of England? Some would look with hopefulness to the Lambeth Conferences as being the nearest in style and structure to an ecumenical council of the Anglican Communion. But we must be careful here. The Lambeth Conference has been defined as 'the regular decennial Conference of Anglican Bishops meeting in private for common counsel . . . No account is ever issued of the speeches and debates, but the Resolutions, Encyclical Letters, and Reports of the Committees [are] published at the time, and are accessible in the official Report'.[1] It is not, that is to say, a 'standing conference' to be appealed to in times of crisis; nor has it ever regarded its findings to be binding on the whole Anglican Communion in the sense that the documents of Vatican II are prescriptive for Roman Catholics.

In 1897, Randall Davidson, then Bishop of Winchester, wrote to the Bishop of Albany in the United States to say that 'the idea of some central tribunal of reference, for disputes on doctrinal or even disciplinary questions, has got a firm hold on the minds of very many ... Colonial and Missionary Bishops'. He was sorry, however (he continued) that he had not realized how unpopular such a suggestion had been in other parts of the Anglican Communion, notably, 'in *your* branch of our Church, a branch eminently capable of taking care of itself'.[2]

In our own day, the Anglican Consultative Council (with its own Doctrine Commission) is undoubtedly looking for a greater sense of unity among the provinces of the Anglican Communion. But it would still be basically incorrect to say that the Lambeth Conference is for Anglicans what the Second Vatican Council has been and continues to be for Roman Catholics. We must therefore look elsewhere for the seat of authority in the Church of England.

Historians will remind us that the authority vested in the papacy of the Middle Ages was, at the time of the English Reformation, transferred not to the Archbishop of Canterbury but to the Crown. Today, the ultimate authority in the Church of England still resides legally in the Queen in Parliament.

To many this sounds an act of sheer godlessness, until it is remembered that medieval theology (to which the Reformers were the direct heirs), saw the whole of society, sacred and secular, temporal and spiritual, as being embraced in a single divine order. The Reformers took this a stage further. For them, kings were 'by God appointed' and the 'Lords of the Council and all the Nobility' were responsible not only for the 'punishment of wickedness and vice' but also for the 'maintenance of true religion and virtue'. Parliament thus became integral to the decision-making of the Church of England, not simply in matters of administration and internal discipline, but also in matters of faith.

One of the most important Acts under the new scheme of things in the sixteenth century was the prescribing of the use of the *Book of Common Prayer* for the whole realm (in 1549 and again in 1552, 1559 and 1662). This in itself was highly significant since the Prayer Book is much more than a form for services and sacraments, containing in its compass the whole doctrine of the Christian religion as understood and interpreted by the Reformers.

When in 1927, Parliament was once more asked to consider the most far-reaching revision of the Prayer Book since its original composition, many were scandalized at the thought of a body which by then consisted of men of a variety of religious allegiances and some of none, rejecting the wishes of regular worshippers (as represented in the Church Assembly) by a narrow majority in the Commons (238 to 205 in the first debate and 266 to 220 in the second). But at the same time there were those (as the 1970 report *Church and State* observes) who regarded themselves as better represented in religious matters by the House of Commons than by the Church Assembly',[3] and Parliament has continued to be trusted.

Today, the Alternative and Other Services Measure, passed through Parliament in 1965, ensures that the Church of England (through the General Synod) may propose services alternative to or additional to those provided by the *Book of Common Prayer* and authorize their use by canon. But Parliament remains the final authority and, as we shall see, the General Synod itself owes its own authority solely to that delegated to it by Parliament.

Why then, it will be asked, are the controversies which vex the Church of England not debated in Parliament which alone has legal authority to settle them? The answer is that on the one hand, there is no time in the Parliamentary schedule (as archbishops and bishops have frequently been told), nor would it be likely that members of either the Upper or Lower House would in all good conscience embark on a debate, for example, on Christian doctrine. There are, after all, other forums set up or authorized by Parliament so that the Church may debate and propose legislation for its own concerns.

There are first the Convocations of Canterbury and York, which are ancient bodies that grew out of the English local con-ciliar system of the Middle Ages. The Upper House of each Convocation consists of all the bishops of the province, the Lower House of senior and representative clergy. At the time of the Reformation, both Convocations made an act of submission to the Royal Supremacy and from that time onwards met at the beginning of each new Parliament, being summoned by the sovereign himself (as today the Queen summons the General Synod). Parliament therefore still had the overall authority, and this was readily admitted by the Church. In Richard Hooker's view, for example, Convocation was a body 'best suited for dealing with the technicalities of public worship'; but (he goes on to say), 'the King in Parliament alone can give such regulations the force of law',[4] meaning that the Convocations have no final authority, as is the case today.

By 1742, the Convocations were no longer summoned. They were revived in 1852 and 1861 respectively; and by 1885 each had a House of Laymen attached in an advisory capacity. They met for the first time together (with the Houses of Laymen) in 1904 as the 'Representative Council of the Church of England'; and in 1919, by the Enabling Act of that year, the National Assembly of the Church of England was set up (thereafter called the Church Assembly), its members consisting of both houses of the two Convocations with a House of Laity elected every five years from the members of diocesan conferences. The new Assembly did not replace the Convocations, but met about three times a year to 'deliberate on all matters concerning the Church of England and to make provision in respect thereof'.[5] Despite this apparently all-embracing agenda, it was not allowed to pronounce on matters of theology and therefore spent a good deal of its time preparing ecclesiastical measures for transmission to Parliament. Theology had to be left to the Convocations.

In 1919, therefore, authority in matters of faith apparently lay with the Convocations which had as their function 'to legislate by Canons in matters ecclesiastical' and 'to determine doctrine, liturgy and ceremonial' while the Church Assembly handled the administrative questions which needed to be negotiated through Parliament. But as we have seen, the Convocations had nothing like so free a hand as might be supposed. They could only meet when summoned by the sovereign. They could neither constitute nor execute canons without the Royal Assent. Nothing they determined could be against the prerogative of the king, the common law, the statute law or any custom of the realm. Nor could they infringe the Act of Uniformity (which imposed the Prayer Book) and by implication could say nothing contrary to the Thirty-Nine Articles of Religion which were similarly protected by Act of Parliament.[6] The Convocations were instructed by the Crown during the years preceding the 1927 Prayer Book debate to consider the matter in question; but the final legislation had to come from Parliament, and Parliament alone.

There were however (and still are) the Church courts. From medieval times, each diocese in the Church of England has been provided with a consistory court, through which the bishop of the diocese administers ecclesiastical law with the assistance of his chancellor (who in fact presides over the court). Clergy may be arraigned before such courts on charges of either personal misconduct or erroneous teaching. Appeal is allowed from the diocesan court to the provincial courts (the Court of Arches for Canterbury and the Chancery Court for York) and from these to the final court of appeal, the Judicial Committee of the Privy Council. Matters of personal indiscipline on the part of the clergy have proved by and large easier to deal with than those of doctrinal error. It is much simpler, for example to deprive a clergyman found guilty of adultery, where the evidence is plain, than to decide against a priest who claims that he is expressing traditional doctrine in a new way which does not at first sight correspond to the formularies of the Church.

The best-known use of the Church courts is probably their summoning in the late nineteenth century for the examination of clergy charged with ritual offences. Those clergy imprisoned after being found guilty of liturgical uses not authorized by the Church of England were not in fact sentenced for the offence itself but for contempt of court, shown through their refusal to desist. But two interesting points emerge. First, when Edward King, Bishop of Lincoln, was found guilty on two charges (mixing the chalice and making the sign of the cross in absolution), the Judicial Committee of the Privy Council gave wholehearted support to the Archbishops' court, not judging itself competent to declare against such clear evidence on what must be admitted was a very petty matter.[7] And second, after the Royal Commission on Ecclesiastical Discipline of 1906 had made its report it was declared that in matters which were controversial and not clearly defined in the formularies of the Church of England, 'such questions shall be referred to an assembly of the Archbishops and Bishops of both Provinces ... and the opinion of the majority of such assembly of the Archbishops and Bishops ... shall be binding on the Court for the purposes of the said appeal'.[8] In other words, a secular court believed itself incompetent to pronounce on questions which could only be resolved by those who held an authority inherent in their office if not legally final in the Church of England.

Other matters, such as allegations of doctrinal error, were more difficult to judge. In 1864, a Church court could sentence two clergymen to deprivation (H. B. Wilson and R. Williams) for their opinions in a volume of liberal theology, *Essays and Reviews*, in which they were said to deny the inspiration of Scripture and the possibility of eternal damnation.[9] In this century, however, archbishops have been much more cautious. Archbishop Fisher wisely resisted the suggestion that he should try Bishop Barnes of Birmingham for his apparently unorthodox views on the resurrection; and in the so-called 'Honest to God' debate, there was no suggestion from any official quarters that Bishop Robinson should be put on trial, nor has it ever seemed likely that the bishops today would attempt to quiet the fears of the Christian public by dragging liberal and controversial clerics before the justices. Yet the courts remain, powerless of course to make a judgement in any way contrary to the formularies of the Church of England but nevertheless a forum in which a bishop, after due consultation, may decide whether a cleric accused of false doctrine may continue to teach or not. In so doing he declares by implication what true doctrine is.

A much more promising arena for debate and decision-making in the Church of England is the modern General Synod. The General Synod of the Church of England came into being in 1969. It was not an entirely new body, but basically 'the Church Assembly, given the functions and authority of the Convocations'.[10] The Convocations themselves met to pass canons (with the Royal Assent) delegating their authority to the new assembly; and though the General Synod is subject to the same restrictions in law as those limiting the powers of the Convocations, for the first time the Church of England has a freedom to debate and decide upon its own affairs without constant recourse to Parliamentary machinery. Canons still require the Royal Assent before promulgation, and there have been occasions when Parliament has refused to approve a Measure giving the General Synod power to make such canons as it wishes to submit for the Royal Assent. But it is now much easier to see the Church of England in its appointed and elected representatives debating and legislating for its members and achieving results more effectively and with less delay.

Unlike the Church Assembly, the General Synod is authorized to debate matters of doctrine, worship and the administration of the sacraments. In this the House of Bishops has a special role. Any proposed alteration to the existing forms of service, any matter touching Christian doctrine, any matter which is related to both theology and discipline (e.g. the marriage service) must, before the final debate at which a vote is taken, be referred to the House of Bishops. The House of Bishops in turn will then resubmit the proposal to the General Synod in terms drawn up by the bishops alone. The matter is then debated and a vote taken, normally requiring a two-thirds majority in each house before it becomes law.[11] The proposal may of course be defeated, and there is no question of the bishops having their own way on doctrine and allowing the rest of the Synod to deal with practicalities. The aim is to hear the voice of the whole Church through its representatives. But it is significant that on such occasions, the Church looks to its bishops for particular guidance as it does in so many other instances. For in the search for the location of authority within the Church of England, the bishops of the Church are clearly prominent in each area that has been examined.

It is the bishops who meet at Lambeth, it was the bishops and representatives of the ordained ministry who formed the original convocations, it was the bishops who were called into consultation by the king and Parliament from a time well before the Reformation, it is the bishop who decides on the use of the Church courts, it is an assembly of bishops and archbishops who may decide matters on which the Judicial Committee of the Privy Council feels incompetent to pass judgement, and it is the diocesan bishops who are *ex officio* members of the General Synod and exercise a special role in the determining of Christian teaching. Somehow, through the web of bureaucracy, democracy and establishment, the historic role of the bishop as guardian of the Christian tradition and as representative and spokesman of the whole Church emerges with considerable strength.

The Church of England is after all an episcopal Church. Traditionally, and in other episcopal communions, it is the bishops as leaders and representatives of their churches who meet in council to share common concerns and to resolve disputes over doctrine and discipline. They do not of course act without reference to the opinions of the whole Church, clerical and lay, which they have taken care to consult; nor when they pronounce on any matter do they expect immediate agreement from the rest of the Church, since their decisions have to be received, considered and may even be corrected by the response of Christendom as a whole. But this is their traditional role and all episcopally governed churches must expect their bishops to be called to exercise this kind of authority when needed.

That the bishops of this country before the Reformation did not have theology high on their agenda is probably an indication that they were used to theological matters being settled by more universal synods and were therefore content to accept the frankly secular business before them when the first Convocations met. At the Reformation, however, they were suddenly called to exercise a much more traditional role. Worship and doctrine now had to be decided upon locally – a burden which had rarely been placed on any provincial synod since the time before the great ecumenical councils.

Though from the very beginning the powers of bishops were severely limited by the king and Parliament, and are still limited by the laws governing the General Synod today, in practice it is still the bishops who bear the final responsibility, since they are effectively leaders in all of the forums where decisions affecting the belief and practice of the Church of England have to be made. Parliament may occasionally say them nay, and the General Synod may have powers which it is difficult to justify theologically, but one cannot escape the sense that deep within the mind of the Church of England – as in Anglicanism as a whole – final responsibility is believed to lie with the bishops.

In what follows we shall be looking at the theological constraints which at once limit and support the bishops of any Church in the process of forming judgements about Christian faith and practice. Enough has been said for the time being about the constitutional and legal restraints peculiar to the Church of England. Even though the structures of state and synod may be regarded as no serious threat to episcopal initiative the bishop of any Church still works under other aspects of authority. On the one hand there is the belief of Christendom as represented in Scripture and in its interpretation in tradition. On the other hand there is the living authority, not only of his own immediate communion but of many other communions and federations of churches. He relates to the first of these authorities (Scripture and tradition) in virtue of his leadership of a local church (or diocese) in which Christians daily seek to understand and reinterpret the faith that has been committed to them. He relates to the second (living) authority (firstly to his own communion) as representative of his own church who joins with his fellow bishops in the exploration of Christian truth to which each local church has a contribution to make. The divisions of Christendom today do indeed make such an operation more difficult. There is no single council for the universal Church, nor has there been for many centuries. But for the bishops of the Church of England, the Anglican Communion is now an established reality and the processes of mutual consultation within that communion infinitely more sophisticated than even a decade ago. In addition the Ecumenical Movement is now so far advanced with nearly sixty inter-confessional dialogues in operation that it is hard for any one Church completely to ignore the insights of those with whom it has not immediate communion or episcopal fellowship. There is in other words no such thing as 'the faith of the Church of England' nor even 'the faith of Anglicanism'. We can only properly speak of 'the belief of Christendom'; and in the task of interpreting that faith to the twentieth century, keeping it true to its foundations yet open to its many possibilities, the bishops of the Church of England – with the leaders of other churches – have a continuing and significant role. It is that role which we must now examine.

2 The Bishops, Scripture and Tradition

Most of the letters arriving on a bishop's desk, protesting that one of his colleagues or some other clerical theologian has made a public denial of the faith, contain two objections in common. The first is that the offending statement is 'unscriptural' and the second that it is 'not what Christians believe' (and here the creeds may be quoted, meaning that the statement is out of step with Christian tradition). The bishop receiving such letters is immediately reminded of the fact that in any judgement or statement he may make in reply, he himself as a bishop must look to all aspects of authority in the Church. Scripture is heard by all and read by many; and Christian conviction is both formed and retained by the day-to-day life of the many Christian communities in his diocese and beyond. He can say nothing that will convince, in other words, without reference to what is contained in Scripture, and to what is believed in the living tradition of contemporary Christendom.

First as to Scripture. In common with the other churches of the Reformation, the Church of England declared at the time that 'Holy Scripture containeth all things necessary to salvation: so that whatsoever is not read therein, nor may be proved thereby, is not to be required of any man, that it should be believed as an article of the Faith, or be thought requisite or necessary to salvation' (Article VI of the Thirty-Nine Articles of Religion). It must be noted that this is in no sense a declaration of a fundamentalist approach to Scripture. The fundamentalist position (so called from a movement stemming from the United States at the beginning of this century, among whose adherents the literal inerrancy of Scripture was only one of the 'fundamentals' of the faith), has never been characteristic of the Church of England as a whole, though in Evangelical circles, a high view of the inspiration of Scripture is normal. Already in the sixteenth century it was becoming clear to Anglican thinkers that it was dangerous to '[attribute] unto Scripture more than it can have' (Hooker);[1] that one could not '[leave] every man to make any thing of any text, upon any device out of his own head, to the founding any new and strange doctrine or practice, as necessary therefrom, or *to the opposing of any constantly received doctrine or practice of the Church universal*' (Peter Gunning).[2] The real meaning of the Article was that the Church 'requires nothing to be believed, as an article of faith, or as necessary to Salvation, but *what the Apostles first taught*, and what *the Church of Christ* in all ages hath believed to be *consonant to the doctrines contained in their writings*'(William Beveridge).[3] Scripture, moreover, was not to be regarded as 'a body of law like those on our English Statute Book wherein it is the legislator that all the way speaks to the people, but as a collection of very different sorts and written at very different times' (Robert Boyle).[4] And in the appeal to Scripture, Christians using their reason to 'judge the sense' must do so not as mere individuals but be regulated 'part by the principle of faith, partly by Tradition, partly by Catholic maxims of her own [i.e. reason's own internal principles]' (Daniel Whitby).[5]

The appeal to Scripture is therefore very much more complex than at first appears. One basic fact emerges, namely that the Scriptures of the Old and New Testaments have never in the tradition of the Church of England been regarded as the single controlling factor in the establishment of Christian truth. The reverence which the early Church paid to the Scriptures, reading them at length, carrying them in procession with lights and incense, laying them open at ecumenical councils and on the nape of a bishop's neck at his ordination all might suggest that men sat under Scripture in obedience to the written word. A similar view could be taken of Reformation and post-Reformation attitudes in a world in which some medieval teachings and practices that could not be found in nor supported by Scripture were swept aside. 'If the Pope acts contrary to the Scriptures,' wrote Martin Luther, 'we are bound to stand by the Scriptures to punish and to constrain him ...'[6] But though the Fathers of the early Church, like those of the Reformation, invariably quoted Scripture in support of their opinions and convictions, it would not be true to say that a new insight from the reading of Scripture *by itself* was the sole warrant for an adjustment to traditional formularies or practices. Luther's new and dramatic apprehension of the doctrine of justification by faith, for example, was not simply based on a chance reading of St Paul. He himself admits that he 'did not learn all [his] theology at once', and his *Lectures on Romans* in which the doctrine of justification is a primary concern, contain 'still much of traditional orthodoxy and of St Augustine'.[7] For the discovery, when it came, is only conceivable against the background of a Church which had long understood the significance of the divine initiative in man's salvation and the freedom of God's gift of himself to man. What Luther's study of the Scriptures had achieved was the rediscovery of a true emphasis in the traditional doctrine of grace which had been threatened with obscurity by current medieval devotion and discipline. The Reformation doctrine was in accordance with the Scriptures and rooted in the Scriptures; but it was not the study of the true meaning of the Scriptures alone which dictated the new emphasis.

Others, however, at the time of the Reformation attempted programmes of reform which were not merely in consonance with Scripture but which were seemingly dictated to them by the text itself. Calvin's restructuring of the Church's ordained ministry at Geneva is one example. His authority here is Ephesians 4.11, where the author of the epistle says that among the gifts of the ascended Lord to the Church were the ministries of apostles, prophets, evangelists, pastors, teachers, governments and helps. Calvin believed that by his time the first three of these had become extinct. This left pastors and teachers, often in his writings considered a single office, as the ordinary ministers of a local congregation, elected and ordained by the laying on of hands by other local pastors. 'Governments' he appointed as 'seniors (i.e. elders) selected from the people ... pronouncing censures and exercising discipline'; and 'helps' were to be deacons, divided into two classes, 'those who gave and those who showed mercy (i.e. Almoners and Guardians of the poor)' *Institutes* IV.3.9.).[8] In this he clearly felt that he was reinstating the practice of the apostolic Church as witnessed in Scripture, from which later Christendom has sadly deviated. So much, we may say, for a sixteenth-century Reformed attitude to Scripture.

But there are even today a good many arguments about bishops (or 'episcopacy') not being 'of the essence' of the Christian ministry, but an expedience brought in at the turn of the first century, which are based on *what may or may not be proved from the text of Scripture*. The reasoning, simply stated, is that if 'mon-episcopacy' (i.e. the pattern of one bishop in charge of a local church) is 'non-scriptural', then the absence of this pattern of oversight (including the title 'bishop') in the free churches should be no barrier to their reunion with episcopal churches, since the free churches may well possess a form of ministry more ancient and more democratic than that adopted by the Church at the very end of the New Testament period. Dr J. I. Packer for example, commenting on the Anglican–Methodist proposals for unity, writes that 'historic episcopacy is completely without foundation in the New Testament. That an episcopal ministry has value, other things being equal, as a sign of unity, continuity and authority of Christ's church is undoubtedly true; but to suspend full fellowship at the Lord's Table on *non scriptural* requirements, those or any other, is sectarian and wrong.'[9]

Higher criticism of the Bible can also lead to similar questionings both in the sphere of doctrine as in that of morals. Much modern questioning of traditional expressions of belief in the incarnation and the resurrection, for example, is the consequence of nearly two hundred years of painstaking research into the actual text of Scripture. For many today, it is no longer true to say that 'The Three Creeds, *Nicene* Creed, *Athanasius's* Creed, and that which is commonly called the *Apostles'* Creed, ought thoroughly to be received and believed: for they may be proved by most certain warrants of holy Scripture' (Article VIII of the Thirty-Nine Articles). For some, Scripture understood correctly in the light of modern criticism will not yield such a portrait of the person and work of Christ as is contained in the creeds, and we must therefore be content with what is presented to us by the evidence in the light of rational investigation. Maurice Wiles, for example, writes in *The Remaking of Christian Doctrine*:

It is essential that the doctrinal theologian recognizes the real position with which he has to deal. He has to recognize that the kind of information about Jesus that theology has so often looked to New Testament scholars to provide is not available. And this is not because those scholars are being over-sensitive or unnecessarily sceptical. The information the theologian has traditionally looked for is simply not the kind of information that can properly be expected to be drawn from the evidence at our disposal by historical means. This is something the theologian has simply to accept. There is nothing noble, magnanimous or radical about his doing so. Like Carlyle's interlocutor who said she had decided to accept the universe, he has in fact no option if he wishes his theology to be concerned with the real world and not with some fantasy world of his own creation.[10]

There are similar problems in the sphere of moral theology. Many moral theologians, for example, will say that the teaching of Jesus about the indissolubility of marriage is unequivocal and witnessed to in the text of Scripture (Mark 10 and Matt. 19). From the earliest times, Christian casuistry has found exceptions to the rule (e.g. St Paul permits the believing partner to separate from the unbelieving partner if conversion does not take place, 1 Cor. 7.15); and today there is a complete list of impediments to a valid marriage which are invoked as grounds for dissolution from the bond. Some, however, will point out that in St Matthew's record Jesus makes an exception to the rule and allows a man to put away his wife and marry another should his wife have been convicted of unchastity (Matt. 19.9). If this is a valid tradition (and there may be no reason to suspect that it is not), then cannot the Church today allow a similar exception and remarriage in church of those whose partners have been divorced from them on grounds of adultery? Whatever commentaries may say about this part of the text representing a 'relapse into the assumptions of surrounding Judaism',[11] any intelligent Christian who believes that Scripture must condition what the Church believes and does might urge an immediate reform of current Church practice! But the Church, least of all the Church of England, does not react in this way. The tradition of Christendom is that marriage is for life; and exceptions to this are worked out not on the basis of the one exception clause in Scripture,[12] but on a variety of other considerations about the nature of marriage itself (i.e. impediments to the original bond or, as for some in the Church of England today, the 'death' of the first marriage).

There must be many biblical scholars today who are not only disappointed but dismayed by the Church's seeming reluctance to absorb into its regular teaching the clear findings of sound scholarship. Little of modern criticism seems to have penetrated the catechism, clergy in their preaching are either unadventurous or plain ignorant, and there is absolutely no hope at present of even a minor adjustment to the creeds. At the other end of the scale there are also those in the Church of England who want liberal theology which questions the 'virgin birth' and the 'bodily resurrection' to be met with the same kind of counterblast that swamped the Roman Catholic Modernists in the time of Pius X. Some have even gone so far as to ask the bishops to take the equivalent of an 'oath against modernism' by asking for straight factual answers to what they believe to be straight historical questions. The bishops, mercifully, have remained impervious to such appeals. Characteristically the Church of England is taking time to absorb the impact of modern biblical scholarship and will hopefully in due course produce a constructive response, as it did to the scientific discoveries of the last century. What the Church is not going to say, however, is that (to use a geological metaphor) 'if the Bible shifts, the Church cracks', because the Bible in this sense is not foundational to the Church. The Church is built on the revelation by God to a community in a Person who brought salvation, and it is this community which has ever since had the task of interpreting this experience to the world of its own time. Its earliest attempts at interpretation are preserved for all time in Scripture, in itself, under the light of modern criticism, a fairly shifting sand, though possessing a coherence and authenticity (once the canon of Scripture was formed) to make it indispensable in the life of the Church as a primary witness to the foundations of the faith. New light on Scripture should of course always feed the community's continuing reflection on its own beliefs and proclamation, but this cannot be the only spur to reconsideration. Should, for example, biblical scholarship inform us that the accounts of the resurrection appearances in Matthew, Luke and John are basically unhistorical and that St Mark's account (without 'the lost ending' of 16.9–20) is the only one we can trust, then we could well conclude that the story of Jesus ends with an empty tomb, a stolen body, some frightened women and a vague promise for a young man that 'He is risen'. But we have also to contend with the tradition inherited by St Paul (in 1 Cor. 15) that Jesus 'died ... was buried ... was raised ... and that he appeared', and with a community which willingly included the resurrection narratives of Matthew, Luke and John, fully historical or not, as being reliable testimonies to what Christians believed and experienced. Here again, we are relying not on the Book by itself but the Book and the community which wrote it. This means that we must now examine more carefully what is meant by tradition.

The first ARCIC statement, *Authority in the Church*, originally published in 1976, opens with a consideration of this subject.[13] Central to the understanding of this, or indeed of any other of the Commission's statements, is the notion of *koinonia*, a Greek term sometimes translated 'fellowship' but better perhaps 'communion' and meaning the life that mankind enjoys in fellowship with its Creator and the companionship that one human being searches for in another and with the rest of human kind. The author of the first epistle of St John, for example, explains to his readers that his purpose in writing and telling them about the revelation in Christ is 'so that you may have fellowship [communion] with us; and our fellowship [communion] is with the Father and with his Son Jesus Christ' (1 John 1.3). The whole purpose of God's revelation in Christ is 'to create a communion of men with God and with one another'; and the Church, which itself is such a communion, exists solely to serve God's purposes in bringing the whole human race into a single communion and fellowship.

God's first act through Christ was therefore to bring into being a communion, a fellowship of men and women, starting with Christ's earthly family, his friends, his neighbours, his disciples – culminating finally with the twelve whom he chose and appointed, who lived with him, learned from him, wondered about him, had ambiguous feelings about him, but who in the end recognized that in him God had brought salvation to all mankind. This was a very gradual process of apprehension. Whatever is recorded in the Gospels of what Jesus said about himself, the final portrait is that of the earliest Christian community. There was never any occasion when the apostles had dictated to them a charter for the Church. They had only at their disposal the Scriptures of the Old Testament, the Life which they observed and reflected on, and their own communion with God through the ordinances and worship of their religion. After the resurrection it was the community and the community alone which had to explain to existing Judaism that with the coming of the Messiah a new departure in their history had been made, that a new Israel had been inaugurated and that far from destroying the ordinances of the old Israel, the new would restore its life in a manner which had been long awaited. Water had been turned into wine, a crumbling pile into a living temple, slavery into freedom and the dead weight of a guilty conscience into the joyful service of a living and ever-present King and Messiah.

For a period of time which we cannot accurately measure, this faith was believed and practised first in a single community which attracted many, then in a series of communities as the apostles moved out from Jerusalem and established the churches of Palestine, Syria, Asia Minor and beyond. It was in these communities that the memory of Jesus was preserved – memory in the sense of traditions about him, stories about him, stories told by him, paradigms, sayings and above all the narrative of his death and resurrection. All this has been scientifically explored by the form-critical tradition in New Testament scholarship and has left us with a vivid picture of a living faith growing in a living environment. It is quite clear that the 'memory' of Jesus was almost always spoken of in a context of interpretation – a story about Jesus, for example, might be told in order to evoke faith in Jesus – and it is this interpretative element which makes it difficult to recover what could have been the original form of the narrative or saying. No matter. The oral traditions of the earliest communities of which we have glimpses in the Acts and epistles represent the community at work, reflecting upon the meaning of Jesus for the new Israel and the communication of this truth to the Gentile world.

Communities, of course, could be at variance with one another both about Jesus himself and about the mission of the Church. The church at Colossae, for example, was clearly in trouble with variants of the Christian message (Col. 2.8); and the conflict at Jerusalem about the admission of the Gentiles without circumcision, involving both Peter and Paul, had to be settled to prevent serious division (Gal. 2, cf. Acts 15). There is indeed considerable variety in the primitive Church's understanding of its faith, but at the same time there are limits, and it is the community with its leaders that in each case draws the line. The Scriptures, as they came to be written, illustrate the richness and variety of the earliest Christian proclamation; but they also tell the story of the struggle to maintain coherence and communion among the churches. The formation of the canon of the New Testament, itself in response to the challenge of Marcion and others, reveals a gravitation rather than an organized movement towards an orthodoxy which, though comprehensive, well knew where false teaching could do damage.

The Scriptures of the Church therefore represent the earliest tradition. They are of course unique; they were brought into being by the community which produced the authors, and it is the whole community as well as the author which must be seen as under the guidance of the Holy Spirit in determining their contents. Once having been written, the Scriptures now remain for all time in the Church as the 'normative record of the authentic foundation of the faith'.[14] For centuries the Church – as the continuation of the community which produced the Scriptures – has interpreted this record and lived the faith, and it is by this means that Christianity has penetrated many new cultures (including our own) and has spoken to the modern world of any generation. But there can be no question of seeing the Scriptures on the one hand as one source of revealed truth, and the tradition of church life as another. Both are part of a single stream, the original revelation interpreted in the tradition of the community and recorded in Scripture, and the ongoing life of that same community continuing to interpret the original revelation.

Such a view of Scripture and tradition is fundamental to the Church of England. George Tavard (in *Holy Writ or Holy Church*) shows how the Elizabethan Church fiercely resisted any suggestion of a 'two-source' theory of revelation (some from Scripture, some from tradition) while the Council of Trent, reacting to the 'sola scriptura' cry of the Continental Reformers, nearly made a cardinal error. The first draft of the Council on this subject stated that 'this truth [i.e. of the gospel] is contained *partly* (*partim*) in written books, *partly* (*partim*) in unwritten traditions ... dictated orally by Christ himself or the Holy Ghost and kept in the Catholic Church in continuous succession'. As Tavard notes, '*Equal adhesion of faith is due to both.*' In the final draft, however, the words 'partly ... partly' were omitted and the phrase substituted: 'This truth ... is contained in the written books *and* in the unwritten traditions' (italics mine), logically implying, as Tavard observes, that 'the whole Gospel is contained in Scripture as it is also contained in the traditions'.[15] As for the Elizabethan Church, Tavard continues, it 'has held that the Church and Scripture are always in harmony, Scripture having the primacy because it is the word of God'.[16] Some Anglicans have restricted this harmony to the first five centuries, which explains why the Anglican formularies appeal to the creeds as consistent with Scripture and why Anglican divines quote so frequently from the Fathers of the early

Church. But the logic of the Anglican position remains the same. While proclaiming very firmly the primacy of Scripture, Anglicans have always acted on the principle that 'permanence in revealed truth' is invariably combined with 'continuous exploration of its meaning' and that this in effect is what is meant by tradition. Their conviction is that the same gospel is to be found in the Scriptures as is to be found in the exploration and that the task of exploration is committed to the *koinonia* which lives in fellowship with the Father and the Son through the Holy Spirit.

This being the classical position of the Church of England, then the role of the Church as a whole in exploring and proclaiming Christian truth is paramount. Clearly an immense debt is owed to individuals throughout the centuries who by scholarship, prayer and holiness of life have done much to enlighten Christians' understanding of their faith, and who have often gone ahead in their researches in a way which many find difficult to follow. This is particularly true in our own day when people complain of a gap between what the theologians say and write and what is taught from the pulpit and believed by the majority of Christians. Certainly all must be listened to. But in the last resort, the exploration into Christian truth is a corporate act of the whole Church, because the Church of England like other churches, represents a living tradition, a living communion and fellowship, and the truth of the gospel can only be seen in its wholeness through the community of the Church acting corporately.

The bishop, then, looking at his pile of letters of protest, will have to take all this into consideration. However competent a biblical scholar he may be, Scripture alone will not by itself shape his reply. He may equally have a solid grasp of the Christian tradition; but tradition, as has been shown, is not simply what has been commonly held in the past, but the activity of the living contemporary Church in its exploration of Christian truth. Whatever happens, he cannot act alone, but must always proceed to some form of corporate action before reaching a judgement; and it is this corporate or collegial activity of the bishops that we must next consider.

3 The Bishop's Counsel

The Bishop and the Local Church

Despite appearances of being intrinsically a national Church, the Church of England is in reality and theologically a communion of local churches whose unity and federation has been effected through a variety of causes. Though the prime reason for its present unity may seem to be its establishment under the authority of the Queen in Parliament, the churches of Britain had achieved a sense of commitment to a common cause and an awareness of their mutual interdependence many years before the Reformation. When Archbishop Theodore at the Synod of Hertford in 673 proposed a national synod for the whole English Church to meet at least once a year, he had as one of his motives to bring the Celtic churches into line with Roman usage and thus to establish the whole British Church in harmony with the rest of Catholic Christendom.[1] But at the same time the sheer proposal of synodical meetings meant that he recognized the independent voice of each diocese and the right of all – Celts, Saxons and Romans – to representation. His proposals made little headway and by the time of the Danish invasions, national synods of the Church met no more. After the Conquest, the national importance of each diocesan bishop and his peculiar relationship to the king meant that the unity of the British Church was strengthened by the growing sense of national unity. In this the pope had considerable interest. A united province (by this time two united provinces) would fall more easily under his sway if the shoulders that bore the pallium and the head that wore the crown collaborated in the fight against rivals and insurrection. Pope and king for a long period together appointed to bishoprics and many other ecclesiastical preferments. *Ecclesia Anglicana* was already in the making.[2]

Nonetheless, the importance of the diocesan bishop as leader and representative of his own church was never submerged wholly in the national or papal interest. Individual bishops were a force to be reckoned with. As men of secular as well as ecclesiastical training, they commanded not only considerable wealth but also a temporal authority, which could not be lightly ignored.[3] Provincial synods met only intermittently during the later Middle Ages and usually to deal with the growing pains of the Reformation (in the shape of Wyclif or the Lollards). Doctrinal matters were settled abroad in the ecumenical councils of the Western Church. The Convocations, as we have seen, were called primarily to deal with the taxation of the clergy; only after the Reformation did each bishop of the two provinces attend Convocation on the summons of the king to deliberate the Reformed religion. This was a necessary, but at the same time a shrewd move. Though the bishops, both collectively and individually, had had some of their powers severely curtailed by the Act of the Royal Supremacy, the king could never ignore the fact that a bishop as an individual was of the very fabric of the national hierarchy, and that he represented in his person not simply a view of religion but the political and religious sentiments of some of the most powerful in the land. It made sense for the king to send one bishop, John Fisher of Rochester, to the scaffold for refusing to submit to his supremacy; but it would have been foolhardy of him not to admit the rest to his own most intimate counsel.

The role of the bishop as representative of a constituency is as old as the Church itself. The Second Vatican Council has done much to dispel the view that bishops are merely agents of the pope, dispersed strategically among the churches to secure the maximum of conformity to the rulings of the Vatican. They are in fact the appointed leaders of local churches, elected by the will of the people of those churches and commissioned by divine authority through the sacrament of their ordination. By this act the bishop becomes not merely the voice of the universal Church to his people, but the voice of his people to the universal Church.

This perspective on the bishop is rooted in a rediscovered perspective on the Church.[4] For a long time, a narrow reading of Roman Catholic ecclesiology gave the impression that for Roman Catholics the Church was a single community, presided over at the centre by the pope and administered locally by the pope's delegates, the bishops. The documents of Vatican II, however, suggest that this is too simplistic a portrait. On the one hand they speak of the 'mystery of the Church' (by which they mean God's saving action in Christ which is made present and effective through the Church); and on the other hand they say that this saving mystery is to be found as fully in any local congregation as it is in the whole communion of churches. According to the decree *Lumen Gentium*,

> This Church of Christ is truly present in all legitimate local congregations of the faithful which, united with their pastors, are themselves called Churches in the New Testament. For in their locality these are the new People called by God ... In them the faithful are gathered together by the preaching of the gospel of Christ, and the mystery of the Lord's supper is celebrated, 'that by the food and blood of the Lord's body the whole brotherhood may be joined together'.[5]

This picture of the people of God, gathered round their bishop for the celebration of the Eucharist is one which should hearten any local congregation. God's saving work through Christ is made present for them through the Eucharist; at that very moment in time, they are the Church of Christ in all its fullness. As Gregory Baum comments, 'the entire gift of God is available to us in the local congregation',[6] and an Orthodox theologian writes: 'The Unity and fullness of the church [is] not to be seen in all the local churches put together, nor in their federation, [which had never been a reality] but in each local church.'[7] For the documents of Vatican II (as Emmanuel Lanne suggests) 'never put forward a concrete image of what the church might be above the local level'. They may talk about collegiality and about the universal communion of churches; but none of these wider views of the church 'manifests the catholic and apostolic church any more than does the local community in its eucharistic celebrations'.[8]

Each local church or diocese, therefore, is of unique importance. No one can claim to hear the voice of the Church as a whole without listening to all the churches. Every church has a right to speak, since God speaks through every church. Every church has a right to be heard; every church has a right to be represented; every church speaks through its elected representative and each church's appointed spokesman and representative is its bishop. He speaks for them and not merely to them, as is brought out very clearly by the manner of his appointment.

The ordination of a bishop in the apostolic succession is after all far more than a guarantee to him and to his people that he stands in a line of succession reaching back to the apostles, in virtue of which he has the required grace to perform episcopal functions. In the first place he has to be elected by the local church; the people of the place must be consulted and asked if they really want him as their bishop. Though episcopal elections today in the Church of England are not what would be called 'democratic', the nomination of candidates to the Crown is nevertheless based on far-reaching research in the diocese which needs a new bishop. The formal election of the Crown's nomination by the dean and chapter of the cathedral church (mercifully preserved for us by Parliament) remains a very important sign that the new bishop is not being forced on the diocese but comes with the approval of the people. At the ordination service itself, the candidate is presented to the people and all are asked, 'Is it your wish therefore that he should be ordained?', and their reply, 'It is', sets the seal on the long process which has sought to give the diocese concerned not only a father in God, but a man to represent them and to speak for them.[9]

The heart of the rite of ordination is the laying on of hands with prayer by the presiding archbishop and as many bishops of the province as are able to be present. This form of appointment can be traced back to the New Testament and was used by the apostles themselves in commissioning the senior ministers of new churches who in turn commissioned others (1 Tim. 4.14; 5. 22; 2 Tim. 1.6).[10] 'Apostolic succession' in this sense means the continuity through the rite of ordination of the episcopal ministry today with the original apostolic ministry. But to be ordained in the apostolic succession means much more than to have simply the right pedigree. In the early centuries of Christian history, the Fathers would distinguish between the 'apostolic churches' (meaning those which taught and practised the faith of the apostles) and alternative forms of religious life (taught for example by the Gnostics or the Marcionites). For the Fathers, the existence of a bishop ordained in the apostolic succession was primarily a sign that the church over which he presided was genuinely apostolic and therefore genuinely Christian.[11] If a schismatic or heretical congregation did not possess such a ministry, then it was not to be trusted. St Optatus of Milevis, a fourth-century North African bishop, put the schismatic Church of the Donatists to the test by tracing the pedigree of the bishops of the small Donatist church at Rome. Five bishops up the family tree he could go no further. The last (and first to be appointed), Victor, was 'like a son without a father', a 'pastor without a flock'. He 'succeeded to no one', he was bishop of nowhere. The church which eventually gathered round him could not therefore be considered apostolic, its faith was not that of historic Christianity.[12] By the same token, the emergence in some early church histories of episcopal lists, tracing the succession of bishops in certain churches back to the apostles was, in the light of this theology much more than a record to be displayed on cathedral walls. Such lists were a sign to the faithful that their church and their bishop together held the apostolic faith. It means the same today. No bishop is ordained unless those who ordain him are sure that his life and teaching are in accordance with the faith of the apostles as proclaimed by the contemporary Church; and no bishop is received by the local church without reassurances that he will maintain their historic faith and work with them for its interpretation to the modern world.

The bishop's enthronement is as important in this respect as his ordination. The rule that no bishop can be ordained without a diocese or area over which to preside, and the parallel rule that there cannot be two bishops in one see is much more than a practical expediency. A bishop is chosen by a church, a bishop is given to a church, and from the moment of his enthronement he is committed with them to that church's mission. He is 'their man' and teaches 'their faith'. When in the year 328, Alexander, Bishop of Alexandria, died, controversy over the election of a successor was expected. In the event, the late Bishop's archdeacon, Athanasius, was chosen 'by the vote of the whole people' and was declared 'lawfully appointed, not the man of contrary opinions but *the man of the same faith*'.[13] That, in the light of the doctrinal controversies which plagued Alexandria at the time, was the prime reason for his election. He taught the faith of the people, they could trust him to speak for them. For no one will trust a bishop without a church; God after all speaks through the church, not just through the bishop, and an unseated bishop, however validly ordained, has nothing to bring with him from the people of God. The act of enthronement places the bishop on the *cathedra* of the diocese, the chair from which the faith has been taught since the first missionaries brought it to that city. The modern Christian church expects nothing more and nothing less than that same faith from that same chair.

If therefore, the bishop in his person represents the faith and convictions of the local Church, then he is obviously bound to spend much of his time consulting with the whole body of Christians in his diocese in order to listen with them to what the Spirit is saying to that church. St Augustine, appointed Bishop of Hippo in North Africa in 396, always regarded himself as a servant of the people of God rather than their superior, 'at their feet' rather than 'at their head', a 'fellow learner', a 'fellow servant' and a 'fellow worker', rather than a 'director of their labours in the vineyard'.[14] It is this spirit and this attitude which enables a bishop most closely to keep in touch with what ordinary Christian commitment in the modern world actually involves.

Consulting the Local Church

A bishop's means of consulting with the clergy and laity of his own diocese may at first sight appear to be built into the diocesan structures. He will meet regularly with his suffragan (or area) bishops, with senior clergy (archdeacons and rural deans) and with his elected bishop's council. At least twice a year he will chair the diocesan synod. There will in addition be no shortage of un-solicited letters from every quarter of the diocese, from Christian and non-Christian alike, expressing opinions about him, his clergy, what the Church should be doing, what the Church should not be doing, together with the more constructive communications on social and political affairs. As time goes by, he will have occasion to visit every parish in the diocese; and his engagements which take him outside the strictly ecclesiastical boundaries will help to keep him in touch not only with how those other than church members view the Church's contribution, but also with how the greater part of society is grappling with human and spiritual problems.

There is however a theological dimension to this process of consultation which is sometimes buried in the sheer givenness of a relentless programme of events. The bishop's brief is to consult the whole church, clerical and lay; but without splitting clergy and laity into a hierarchy – the clergy above, the laity below, the clergy to teach and the laity to learn – the fact remains that theologically and in history, the clergy have always held a particular role in the bishop's counsel and that of the laity has been no less individual. The formation of an elected synod of clergy and laity to work with the bishops in managing the affairs of the Church of England and in debating its doctrine and discipline is a comparatively recent development. It must not be allowed to obscure the more historic forms of consultation which still have their value.

First, the clergy. The second order of ordained ministry, today called 'priest' or in some places 'presbyter', was almost certainly not original to the Christian Church at its foundation.[15] The primitive communities were cared for by one or several ministers, called either bishop or presbyter; only eventually did the pattern emerge of one minister called a bishop being responsible for one local church or diocese. The deacon was probably the earliest assistant minister and ranked high in relation to the bishop. Presbyters as distinct from bishops are met with for the first time in large towns such as Antioch or Rome. The problem for the Christian church in conurbations of such size was to provide for a scattered and growing Christian population which could not conveniently be accommodated under one roof even had a suitable building become available. Christians in towns therefore normally met for worship in house churches.[16] The bishop would obviously visit when he could, but normally he appointed a representative to take care of the pastoral needs of each area. It is as representative of the bishop, therefore, that the second order of ministry, now called presbyter, first appears. This is brought out very clearly in the ordination prayers. Early in the third century at Rome, it is recorded that in ordaining a presbyter, the bishop compares him to the elders in the Old Testament who were appointed by Moses and Aaron because their own ministry had become more than they could bear.[17] This is an important emphasis. Presbyters in the early Church were very much 'bishop's men' and felt themselves to be more part of an episcopal team than on permanent secondment to a parish. Nevertheless, once in the parish they enjoyed a marked degree of autonomy. There was nothing prohibited to them and reserved to the bishop apart from the right to ordain. Theirs basically was the *episkope* or oversight of a pastoral area; but at the same time they could never forget that theirs was also a delegated office. If the bishop arrived then they stood down. It is in this sense that they can be looked on as a 'second' order of ministry, the bishop being the first. But presbyters were 'second' not in the sense that they were a new order brought into being with some of the functions of the first order and other character-istics of their own. Properly understood, the presbyterate is simply an extension of the first order from its centre in the bishop of the diocese. There is, that is to say, only one *episkope*, one ministry of oversight, exercised by the bishop and extended through those whom he appoints and ordains to the presbyteral order.

From earliest times, the presbyters of a city or diocese formed the bishop's council. They were known as 'the court or sanhedrin of the presbyters', 'the sacred and venerable bench of the clergy', 'the Church's senate', 'the council of the Church' and 'the bishop's counsellors'.[18] St Cyprian in the third century made a promise to his clergy at the beginning of his episcopate that he would 'do nothing without your advice and the consent of the people'.[19] This was not exceptional. For many years, the town clergy in particular enjoyed privileged access to their bishop. They were his missioners, sat with him in the cathedral church and had the sense of belonging more permanently to the bishop than they did to the parish.

The spread of Christianity into the countryside, however, with the corresponding increase in the size of dioceses meant that regular communication between the bishop and his clergy had to be reorganized. In a small diocese he could still summon them to council; but in a large and scattered medieval diocese (such as Lincoln in this country) he would have to rely on the ancient offices of archdeacon and rural dean for an understanding of the mood of church life at parochial level. Archdeacons in the Middle Ages get a bad press. Their main task was to act as the bishop's delegate in judicial duties over a prescribed area. They were therefore sent abroad to study law in Italy where the heady conditions involved them in some questionable behaviour but no doubt on the 'set a thief to catch a thief' principle this equipped them well to trap the more modest deviants among the clergy and lay folk of this country on their return. 'Is it possible for an archdeacon to be saved?' wrote John of Salisbury in the twelfth century, a sentiment which many a parish priest would have echoed. Nevertheless, archdeacons were well known and very much in evidence. One of their functions was to preside from time to time over meetings of the rural deaneries which fell within their archdeaconry. Archdeacon or no archdeacon, however, rural deanery clergy met regularly and frequently under the rural dean (sometimes as often as every six weeks). Their business was to receive instructions sent to them by the bishop and to debate parochial affairs, ranging from the appointment of a new incumbent to the misdemeanours of the laity. All was reported to the bishop by the archdeacon and recorded in the episcopal registers. There was thus a constant flow of information from parish to palace. However prelatical the bishop, however dreaded or despised the archidiaconal gaiters, however coveted the office of rural dean, the system spoke the theology that counsel between bishop and clergy was of the essence of the Church's life.[20]

This traditional pattern of communication and consultation survives in the Church of England to this day. It is a structure designed to perpetuate and uphold the original bond between the bishop and his clergy and has the advantage of having grown out of theological considerations rather than from mere practical expediency. Most bishops today would admit that their most valuable source of information about clergy and people in their diocese comes from the regular staff meetings with archdeacons and rural deans. Archdeacons and rural deans are after all very much a part of the normal parochial system. Rural deans are always senior incumbents, archdeacons often hold small benefices or a canonry. They are on the ground, they are with the clergy, they meet chapters of the clergy, they attend conferences with the clergy. The archdeacon may visit to inspect a leaking roof but will probably find himself eventually discussing pastoral need. The whole system is admirably designed to keep the flow of information and consultation open. Like all systems, it has its flaws; but it nonetheless reflects the ancient principle that the clergy of a diocese are the bishop's delegates and that they are the bishop's council. Rural deanery chapters may seem a long way from the corridors of power; but they should be looked upon as representative bishop's councils rather than occasions for sharing ecclesiastical gossip and executing a little local business. They are a key factor in the Church's search for an understanding of its mission and for this reason alone should be given a high degree of priority.

Some clergy, however, may consider themselves better represented in the bishop's council be securing election to the diocesan
synod. Synod for some is much more of a platform than the rural
deanery chapter. The bishop is present, all senior clergy are there,
there is a substantial body of articulate lay people and the subjects
for debate are less exclusively parochial and often have a bearing
on the work of the General Synod. Any clergyman may stand for
election, all clergy may vote for the candidate of their choice. It is
here, however, that one basic problem in the whole synodical
system begins to make an appearance. It is true that the clergy on
the diocesan synod are elected from deanery synods and therefore
could be said to represent a broad cross-section of the diocese.
But elections, as is well known, arouse a new interest. It is not
simply a question of choosing a 'reliable man' but a man who will
speak for 'us'. Pressure groups in the electorate itself, therefore,
may successfully put in their own candidate to speak for them (for
or against the ordination of women, for example); but the question
remains, Once elected, does he speak for the deanery from which
he comes or for the pressure group which secured his election?
Without in any sense introducing either a paranoid or over-
dramatic element into this subject, the question has to be asked,
Does an *elected* representative stand for a constituency of *people* or
for a constituency of *opinion*?

The diocesan synod today is fortunately in no sense a substitute
for traditional methods of consultation. Bishops will normally
balance what they hear in synod with what they glean from staff
meetings and parochial visitations. Every clergyman therefore still
has an effective voice in the bishop's council. What has to be
avoided, however, is an ascendancy of the synodical system over
the more ancient and theologically-based structures. Elected
representatives to the diocesan synod may have a comparatively
small impact on the final decisions of the Church of England as a
whole; elected representatives to the General Synod, however,
may contribute to altering the whole course of teaching and
discipline in certain vital areas, thus affecting Church life in every
diocese and at every level. Of these in particular, the same question must be asked, Do they represent constituencies of *people* or
constituencies of *opinion*? If it is mainly the latter, then there will
be considerable numbers of clergy and lay people in the Church
of England who may rightly claim that in the most important

decision-making body of the Church today, their voice has no opportunity to be heard.

It is not always quite so clear how the bishop ought to initiate and develop regular consultation with lay people. Fortunately, we no longer live in a Church where it is for the clergy to teach and the laity to learn – the *ecclesia docens* and the *ecclesia discens* of an earlier generation.[21] The Church which explores Christian truth is the whole people of God; in this process the clergy play only one role, albeit a distinctive one. The layman's role is no less distinctive. Though in the Western Church it has been customary to class Christians as either clerics, religious or laity, this ought never to be regarded as a hierarchy with the clergy at the apex and the laity at the base.[22] All that is meant by this is that the layman is neither a cleric nor a religious, but fulfils a purpose different from that of the ordained and the professed, though no less essential to the total mission of the Church in the world. The Second Vatican Council affirmed that:

> the laity, by their special vocation, seek the kingdom of God by engaging in temporal affairs and by ordering them according to the plan of God. They live in the world, that is, in each and in all of the secular professions and occupations. They live in the ordinary circumstances of family and social life, from which the very web of their existence is woven. Today they are called by God that by exercising their proper function, and led by the spirit of the Gospel, they may work for the sanctification of the world from within as a leaven. In this way they may make Christ known to others ... Therefore, since they are tightly bound up in all types of temporal affairs, it is their special task to order and to throw light upon these affairs in such a way that they may be made and grow according to Christ to the praise of the creator and the redeemer. (*Lumen Gentium* IV.1.)

Since the laity are so much in the forefront of the Church's mission, their unique understanding of the nature of that mission from their peculiar vantage point is indispensable. How therefore may they be best consulted, how actually included in the Church's councils? There have been many attempts at a satisfactory solution. An obvious one is to invite lay people to a council. Before the Reformation, there was a tradition of inviting senior or expert lay people to an ecumenical or provincial synod, but only rarely did they have the right to vote.[23] By the sixteenth century this courtesy was considered by many to be wholly insufficient. The most radical (in the Congregational or Independent tradition) proposed that the Church by its very nature was a 'gathered' congregation, called into being by the Holy Spirit, and that therefore the congregation of lay people was the seat of all authority and had the right to appoint its minister and order the affairs of the local and independent church. It was not, that is to say, so much a question of consulting the laity as of recognizing that the laity were the Church and therefore had to have all powers of decision and judgement in their own hands.[24] Not so the Church of England. The Reformation settlement disappointed many, particularly those returning from overseas, in that there seemed to remain the same degree of prelatical and hierarchical dominance as had obtained before the reign of Elizabeth. But there was a subtle difference.

It has to be remembered in the first place that for centuries, the people of this country have been represented in ecclesiastical affairs by Parliament. Before the Reformation, prince and priest worked in a sometimes uneasy alliance to promote the Christian commonwealth. At the Reformation, this partnership between temporal and spiritual overlords altered significantly. A Bishop of Winchester (Thomas Bilson) wrote at the time, 'The opposite of temporal is not spiritual, but eternal.' Eternal governance therefore belonged to God, temporal to the king and nothing in the shape of the ordering of society to the church.[24] The clergy might preach, administer the sacraments and care for the flock; but all administration of land and law, politics and defence was to be firmly in secular hands. In addition, such was the authority of the king under God, that no ecclesiastical measures could be sanctioned whether they concerned doctrine, worship or administration without their first being presented to the king and the civil magistrates for final authorization. Legally the situation is unchanged today; legally lay people in the Church of England are still represented in church affairs through the House of Commons; legally, it is the whole electorate that has power to restrain the Church if they see the need, or to support and encourage if they think it appropriate. The Church of England did not lose its Proposed Prayer Book of 1927 because Parliament was godless, but because Parliament sincerely believed it was representing the same constituencies in religious affairs that it was accustomed to represent in political and social questions.

The competence of Parliament to represent Christian lay opinion was obviously open to question when non-Christians and Christians of other denominational allegiance were admitted Members after the repeal of the Test Acts in 1828 and 1829. The addition of the Houses of Laymen to the two Convocations was a first step towards researching an authentic lay voice and when these became the House of Laity of the Church Assembly in 1919, there could be no complaint that the laity were unrepresented in the day-to-day running of church affairs. All could attend the Annual Church Meeting, all on the electoral roll could stand for election to parochial church councils, all had opportunity to be nominated or elected to ruridecanal or diocesan conference and from there had an even chance of being able to speak in the Church Assembly. Today, the General Synod by its constitution gives an even more important voice to the laity. Since the Synod (unlike the Church Assembly) has powers to debate doctrine and worship, there is no aspect of Christian living or belief to which the lay person may not bring his wisdom and experience. The system at first sight seems unfaultable. But there are problems.

First (and one that has been met before), do the laity elected to Synod represent constituencies of people or constituencies of opinion? In other words, is the bishop at Diocesan Synod going to be faced with lay people representing pressure groups, or lay people speaking for areas of pastoral concern? This may not be too serious an issue at the level of diocesan or area synod, but assumes far larger proportions in the General Synod. And second, whatever the merits of Synod as a new and manageable forum, does it run the risk of obscuring *traditional* methods of lay consultation? Just as it is possible to listen more attentively to the practised rhetoric of those elected to the House of Clergy and to miss the less articulate wisdom of rural deanery chapters, so it may be that a local church may be persuaded by competent and well-educated laity, chosen for their ability to speak in public, and miss what the greater proportion of lay people, the very heart of church life at parochial level, are actually saying and thinking.

Let us look briefly at the tradition. In the early Church, representations about doctrine and discipline were not infrequently made by the laity. For example, it was Eusebius of Dorylaeum, a prominent layman in Constantinople, who first told the authorities that the people were very uneasy about the sermons of their new bishop, Nestorius, and feared a wholesale attack on their faith and devotion.[26] In that case the bishops gave the laity a hearing, took the matter to council, made a decision and passed this on to the clergy and people of their respective dioceses. This was by no means the end of the affair, because the laity could still 'vote with their feet' and lay indignation at conciliar decisions was certainly not something to be swept under the carpet. There was as much lay solidarity, for example, against the Council of Chalcedon in the Monophysite world as there was European solidarity amongst the Gothic laity against the supporters of the Council of Nicea and Celtic solidarity in Britain against the introduction of Roman customs. Though much of this was for social and political reasons, the bishops ignored powerful lay groundswells at their peril. If they wanted the unity of the churches then they had to bring their churches with them. It was therefore far better for a bishop to arrive at a council with the baptismal creed of his local church which he knew had the assent of the people, than with a volume of his own theological predilections. Selling the council's decisions to his church on return was on the whole more difficult than making them in the council chamber. In this sense, lay opinion in the tradition of the Church has always been very audible.

The Reformation Settlement in the Church of England surprisingly allowed for the same kind of lay reaction. For example, in 1548 the bishops proposed new forms of worship and new criteria for doctrine (the committee which met at Chertsey in September of that year to draft the 1549 *Book of Common Prayer* was entirely clerical). These were proposed to the official lay consultative body (i.e. Parliament) in December of the same year and imposed on the whole country by Act of Uniformity in January 1549. But there was nevertheless a long process of reception, criticism and comment on the part of the Christian populace which stretched well into the reign of Elizabeth I. The laity again voted with their feet. The majority submitted, some opted for the Separatist alternative and set up independent churches, while others bravely struggled to maintain the Roman allegiance. Parliament in 1928, in rejecting the proposed Prayer Book, declared that they were 'voicing the real underlying wish of a majority of Church folk in

England';[27] and the *vox populi* today, with the added advantages of extensive media coverage, is unmistakeable in its comment on the findings of liberal theology and proposals for new discipline and practice. Such has been the traditional method of lay consultation in the Church of England, the bishops (with their consultative bodies) proposing and the rest of the Church responding through all the channels available from Parliament at Westminster to the annual church meeting in the parish hall. In many ways this has served the Church very well.

However, since the setting up of the General Synod, and the election of a House of Laity to join the bishops and clergy sharing the authority to debate and propose legislation for all matters concerning the Church of England – doctrine and worship included – a new element has been introduced. First, the laity are elected – by deanery synods, it must be remembered, and not by the whole Christian populace. Second, they are declared to be representative, but it is doubtful (for reasons already stated) whether they actually represent fully the constituencies that have sent them to Synod (not many churchgoers, for example, if asked on the spot, would know who represents their area in the House of Laity). And third, they have been 'clericalized'. The General Synod in its debates is not proposing *to* the House of Laity and asking for their reaction, but is, like the Convocations before, proposing *with* the laity *to* the rest of the Church. In the traditional pattern of consultation, the laity now stand with the clergy as the framers of new proposals (and in this are obviously a tremendous advantage). But it cannot be said that if the laity vote with the bishops and clergy, this means that the whole of the rest of the Church is in agreement because their elected representatives have voted 'Aye'. The same process of proposal and response by the whole Church must be allowed to take place before the Church can be said to have made a proper discernment in the matter under debate. In this respect, the Church of England still behaves in a very traditional manner and nothing at present, it seems, is likely to alter this state of affairs.

Bishops on their way to a bishop's meeting or General Synod will therefore have much to take with them. Some will travel with the problems of the inner city, others with those of the Church in the countryside. All will have with them the agonies of the divorced seeking remarriage, the breakdown of clerical marriages, the cause of women seeking ordination to the priesthood, the popularity or lack of it of the *Alternative Service Book* and the reactions of Christians to government policies and problems of industrial relations. But they will also come armed with the advice of the clergy and the voice of the laity, solicited and unsolicited; and it is this which makes the bishop most effectively a guardian of the faith and a father to his people.

4 The Bishops' Council

The Bishop in Council

The role of the bishop as representative of his local church on provincial synod or ecumenical council has a history which reaches far back into antiquity. Already in the New Testament period, it was axiomatic that no local church might continue to be recognized as authentically Christian without clear lines of communication and consultation with other local churches. The gospel that Paul and Barnabas preached to the Gentiles had to be shown to be consonant with that which Peter and James and the elders taught in Jerusalem. When disunity threatened, the apostles and the elders met to frame a discipline and policy which ensured that the Gentile churches would not drift into a new sectarianism but become firmly grafted into the new Israel (Gal. 2; Acts 15). Assemblies of church leaders were to become a familiar feature of the life of the early Church. To begin with, bishops travelled little further to confer with their colleagues than the capital city of the Roman province in which they served. In the year 306 for example, the bishops of Spain, meeting at Elvira, considered themselves perfectly competent to deal with the evident unpopularity of the seventh commandment in their territory without recourse to the universal Church.[1] Later, however, there were graver issues which disturbed not only the peace of the Church but provoked civil unrest in many parts of the empire. The first ecumenical council (Nicea, 325), was therefore called not by bishops, but by an emperor, Constantine the Great, concerned to restore order. The fact that he chaired the council did not mean that he claimed the final word in theological judgement, but merely that he was anxious that bishops should live peacably in their sees without the hatred, enmity and violence that surprised and scandalized so many in the pagan and Christian world alike. Nonetheless, the strategy had the advantage of assembling church leaders who might otherwise never have met, and of enabling the separate provinces of the Church to declare to the empire as a whole the faith which they held in common.

In all synods and councils, the bishops played the leading role. From the earliest times, other clergy and laity were also present, but though they had a voice in the consultations, they were rarely permitted to vote. Lay and presbyteral signatories are evidenced in some of the councils of the later Middle Ages;[2] but the proceedings of the Council of Trent and of the First Vatican Council make it perfectly clear that the primitive discipline should prevail. Doctors of theology might inform the discernments of the bishops. But if the bishops, when they voted, ventured where no sane theologian would normally dare to tread, the experts had to suffer in silence and reserve their criticisms for a later occasion.

The theological reasons for this are self-evident. The councils of the Church's bishops have never in history been a forum for purely academic debate. Their main purpose has been to provide occasions for the sharing and exploration of the common faith of the churches, and each bishop contributes to the council not simply his own personal understanding of the Christian religion but the corporate belief of the people of his diocese. This is no easy task, since though there may be an underlying coherence which unites the parishes and the people whom the bishop represents, the *vox populi* has many different cadences and discord may often be taken for a flouting of the rules of harmony. There will be those, for example, who will welcome with relief the view of some New Testament scholars that there is no factual foundation in the biblical narrative for belief in the virginal conception of Jesus; whereas for others there is no other way of proclaiming the good news of salvation through Christ than by affirming that God took flesh of the Virgin Mary and thus became man without the agency of any human father. Both views have to be represented in the council, whatever the bishop's own personal preference. It is for the council to decide whether or not they are compatible, not the individual bishop. But it is the individual bishop, and none other, who must present the full spectrum of opinion in his diocese for consideration in the assembly of his peers.

This does place the bishop with strong intellectual preferences in a difficult position, particularly if he has served a good deal of his ministry in a critical academic environment. The faith of the people whom he meets in his daily contact with parishes and institutions may often seem to him to be so uncritical as to have lost its appeal to or credibility with the vast majority of thinking people who come nowhere near the Church. It will be tempting for a bishop in this position to want to promote reform and to drag the Church out of its archaisms into the use of the language of modern theology. After all, he does, in what some would call his 'liberal' views, represent a constituency of opinion which has a right to be heard, and many of his supporters may be those of his own diocese. What is he to do? Is he to persevere with his fellow bishops and with as much support as he can rally until reason prevails and the Church starts to speak a new language? Or is he to 'restrain the beams of learning' (as Charles Gore said the incarnate Son of God 'restrained the beams of deity'[3]) in the knowledge that few will be able to follow him and many will be offended through sheer incomprehension. Could he in other words, like Synesius of Cyrene[4] (Bishop of Ptolemais in Egypt in the fifth century) simply accept that the majority of Christians talk the language of myth and are unable to ascend the heights of biblical criticism?

None of these solutions is in fact satisfactory. It has to be remembered that there is good historical precedent in the Church of England for men being appointed to bishoprics who in their previous career have sided strongly with views on the Christian religion which the majority in the Church found disturbing or heretical. R. D. Hampden,[5] despite opposition from the Tractarians for his 'watering down' of Christian dogma, was elected first to the Regius chair at Oxford and subsequently to the see of Hereford, which he served with exemplary patience and pastoral care. Frederick Temple[6] was opposed strongly both at the time of his nomination to Exeter and again on his appointment to Canterbury for daring to accept the findings of natural science about the evolution of species. To us who have lived with the theory of evolution for as long as we can remember this last seems incredible. Yet Temple on his appointment as bishop did not demand the resignation of clergy who wanted to burn *On the Origin of Species*. Nor were his personally-held beliefs any barrier to an effective Christian ministry. They were well known and, as time passed, found to be creatively contributory to the Christian understanding of God and his relationship to the world. The solution, therefore, seems to be that a bishop with strong convictions which others hold to be controversial should obviously not conceal them; but at the same time he must realize that his opinions are a contribution to a wide programme of exploration, not a solution which any intelligent person should immediately accept. Only time will tell in what way new insights will be absorbed into the broad stream of Christian truth. No one pioneer digs its channel, and it has many tributaries.

If the bishops in council are therefore to be explorers and not simply guardians of the Christian faith, then, as in any quest for truth, they have to listen to the whole evidence and not simply to that which seems immediately to make sense, although each stands within the process and none can be completely dispassionate on any issue. But the kind of evidence that the bishops receive during the course of their investigations is sometimes very different from that which may be researched in books. For centuries the Church has listened to holy people and mystics, missionaries and martyrs, humble villagers and ladies in high society, solitary scholars at their desks and crowds demonstrating in the streets in order to grasp the voice of Christian truth. There is no lack of such contributions today; but they do have to be received and understood even though they may seem at first not to contribute naturally to the logic of the debate in process. In the year 458, logic might well have persuaded Leo the Great to reopen the Council of Chalcedon in response to Monophysite pressure. In the event he decided against this, not simply on the advice of fellow bishops but with one eye on crowd behaviour in Alexandria (where the patriarch had recently been murdered) and one ear open to the pillar saint, Symeon Stylites, himself scarcely a dogmatic theologian but an unusually deep well of wisdom.[7] In other words, he listened to the totality of what was being said; and the bishop's task is no less today.

The Council of Bishops

Though meetings or councils of church leaders probably go back to New Testament times the earliest of which we have accurate (albeit only fragmentary) information date from the second century. Their origin and purpose is summarized admirably by E. J. Yarnold and H. Chadwick in *Truth and Authority* (a commentary on the 1976 ARCIC agreed statement, *Authority in the Church*).

In the early Church the first councils ... were regional synods which sought to establish a common policy on such questions as the non-recognition of the charismatic Montanist movement or the date of Easter (Eusebius, *Church History* 5.23–4) or the limits of the New Testament canon (Tertullian, *de Pudicitia* 10). At first conciliar action was commoner in the Greek East than in the West. Tertullian says that in the Greek churches of his time, synods were held to examine difficult and profound questions, and that these synods were held in awe by the faithful as a 'representation of the entire Christian name' (*on Fasting* 13). Councils were seen to be especially necessary when scripture was found to be unclear or where texts could be quoted on both sides on a controversial question such as re-admission of apostates and other grave sinners. In the time of Cyprian of Carthage in the middle of the third century the process of synodical consultation and decision was seen as a guarding of the fullness of catholic truth against partial and individual opinion.[8].

To begin with, synods were regional or local and the provincial synod has continued to be a regular feature of church life despite the rise in the fourth century of the great ecumenical councils. In North Africa, for example, in the year 393, a decision was made that the provinces of that area should arrange for their bishops to attend annually a synod at Carthage under the presidency of the senior bishop. This continued until the Vandal invasions of 428. The records show that apart from the declaration of the faith of Nicea and the detailing of the canon of Scripture, the greater part of the debate concerned local affairs into which occasionally was intruded a matter affecting other provinces as well (for example, the teaching of Pelagius). Decisions of such councils were for Africa and by Africa; and though relationships with the Church overseas could never be ignored, Africa did claim the right to handle its own internal affairs and even placed strictures on clergy who appealed over the head of the primate to what they believed to be a higher authority.[9]

However, the provincial synod undoubtedly provided the inspiration and a good deal of the practical experience for the setting up of wider conferences. Interprovincial councils met either nationally (e.g. the African councils), for the eastern empire (e.g. the Council of Antioch, AD 341) or for the West (e.g. the Council of Serdica, AD 343). Eventually there were councils which represented all the major churches of East and West. The matter for debate was considered to be of universal concern and the decisions of ecumenical councils, such as Nicea (325) and Constantinople (381) came to be regarded as normative for the whole Christian Church. As Yarnold and Chadwick write:

The councils of Nicea (325), and to a lesser degree Chalcedon (451), decisive for the doctrines of the Trinity and the Incarnation respectively, soon come to be looked back to as sacrosanct. The other great councils [Constantinople, 381 and Ephesus, 431] were joined with them to constitute a kind of canon, at first of four, then enlarged to seven [Constantinople II, 553, The First Lateran, 649 and Nicea II, 787], a number which was further extended by the Latin West but not by the Greek East. Among the first seven ecumenical councils, the first four have retained a special place because of the gravity of their subject matter.[10]

Following the Great Schism between the Eastern and the Western churches, the Western Church alone has continued a tradition of councils styled 'ecumenical', whose resolutions are held to be binding on all the participating churches. The Eastern churches have never renounced the principle of the need for an ecumenical council and a synodical form of government prevails throughout. But as one author writes:

Another fundamental principle and essential characteristic of the Orthodox Church is its use of the *synodal system*, in both its local and its central administration. This system has been handed down to us from the early Church and we must on no account depart from it. The Ecumenical Council continues to be the supreme administrative authority in the Orthodox Church, but until it becomes possible for such a Council to assemble, the Church as a whole may and should be administered by extra, periodical general councils in which the whole Orthodox Church is represented – not by councils like the 'Pan-Orthodox Conference' held at Constantinople in 1923.

May the divine Founder and Lord of the Church grant that circumstances will soon permit the functioning of this venerable and most valuable institution![11]

An ecumenical council is of course a rare occurrence. It is only summoned when real need demands such an exercise – the settlement of doctrinal dispute (as in the councils of the fourth and fifth centuries) or to review a programme for reform (as in the Council of Trent in the sixteenth century or the Second Vatican Council of our own time). In itself it expresses the truth that all the churches of Christendom are a part of a single communion and fellowship and share and teach the same faith; and though it is tragic that for centuries there has been no truly ecumenical council, the councils of the Western Church have at least upheld the principle that Christianity is proclaimed and upheld by a universal communion of churches which seek to relate to one another in faith and life, rather than by a series of national and provincial bodies with concerns only for their own internal affairs. That Christ is for all nations is a truth built into the charter of the Christian religion at its inception; and concrete expressions of its internationality would seem to be a prerequisite if the role of Christianity in the bringing of God's gift of reconciliation to a divided world is to be seen as at all credible.

Despite the importance of ecumenical councils, national or provincial synods have throughout history in all provinces proved indispensable, not least in these islands. We know little of early Celtic bishops' meetings. But certainly within a short time of the Roman mission under St Augustine, the British churches began to develop a promising programme of synodical activity. The mind behind the synodical movement was undoubtedly Theodore, Archbishop of Canterbury from AD 668–90. He was an Asiatic Greek by birth, studied at Tarsus and at Athens and was recommended for the see of Canterbury while not yet in subdeacons' orders and consecrated by Pope Vitalian in 668. By 673 he had conducted a visitation of the whole of England and was able to summon all the British bishops to a Council at Hertford. His primary concern, as he himself declares (Bede, *History* IV.5.), was for the unity of the churches. To this end he asked first for the assembled bishops to declare their agreement with 'the canonical decrees of the ancient fathers'. These, for Theodore, were contained in an extraordinarily arbitrary collection of canon law (probably that of Dionysius Exiguus), but he chose ten chapters as being of special importance for the churches of Britain. The two most significant are the first which demands that Easter be kept according to the Roman custom (on the Sunday after 'the fourteenth day of the moon of the first month'), thus opposing the Celtic custom and calling all Christians to a united observance; and the seventh, 'that a synod be held twice a year', which the bishops eventually decided should be only once a year and that at Clovesho near London. The second council recorded under Theodore's presidency met at Hatfield in AD 680. It was occasioned by fears in the church of Constantinople that there had been a revival of the teaching of Eutyches (which anticipated the Monophysite position concerning the person of Christ). Theodore used this opportunity to summon the bishops and ask them to declare their allegiance to the faith proclaimed by the first five ecumenical councils (from Nicea I to Constantinople II) and to these he added the First Council of the Lateran of AD 649. The text of the Council declares:

> We the venerable bishops of the island of Britain assembled in conclave at the place which is called in the Saxon language Haethfeld, having the most holy Gospels before us, hereby unite to proclaim the true and orthodox faith. This same faith Our Lord Jesus Christ delivered in the flesh to his disciples ... this is now set forth in the Creed of the holy fathers and by all the sacred General Councils and by the united voice of the accredited doctors of the Catholic Church. We follow them in devotion and right faith ... (Bede, *History* IV.17)

Two very interesting points emerge. The first is that in searching to demonstrate or establish orthodoxy, the bishops of England declare their agreement with the faith as historically set forth in Scriptures, creeds and councils. Creeds and councils they know in themselves bear witness to the apostolic faith as recorded in the Scriptures and taught by the universal communion of churches. But a research into the title deeds of the Christian churches in order to recognize a common faith is an exercise which contributes greatly to present unity. The second point of interest concerns Theodore himself. Conscious as he is of the commission given him by Pope Vitalian and knowing that his own orthodoxy was in question at the time of his consecration, he is very anxious to demonstrate that the British churches not only now conform to Roman customs, but that they also understand their unity with the universal Church through their acknowledgement of the same faith. An ecumenical council with British bishops present seemed unlikely in the foreseeable future; but the British Church's sense of belonging to the worldwide communion of Christendom would be enhanced if it were realized that the gospel proclaimed by the Thames was none other than that taught by the Tiber or in the land between the Tigris and the Euphrates. The tradition in which the British churches stand has therefore both a historical and contemporary dimension. Historically they look back to the charter of their foundation; but a contemporary awareness of their relationship to the living faith of other Christian churches is indispensable to their sense of belonging to a unity greater than their own within the confines of the nation.

It is generally recognized that the synodical movement initiated by Theodore came to an end in the tenth century with the coming of the Danes, much as the African synods were terminated by the Vandals and those in Spain by the Moors. Travel was dangerous, the kingdoms were preoccupied with the usurpers. The Norman Conquest however brought a new unity to the English Church. New dioceses were created, cathedral churches built and bishops enjoyed a special relationship with the king and hence a sense of belonging to one another in a national cause. Local and provincial synods were held but by this time bishops were being summoned to the Witan and were becoming involved in local and national government. When in the thirteenth century the Convocations were summoned for the first time, it was to deal mainly with the representation of the Church in the matter of taxation. However much Archbishop Chichele believed that the Convocations ought to discuss doctrine it is quite clear that in the pre-Reformation assemblies, business prevailed over theology. Local synods (like that of Norwich in 1428) dealt with local heresies; but appeal in all other matters of orthodoxy and discipline was to Rome. Rome by the later Middle Ages had a great many political and financial fingers in a great many English ecclesiastical pies. Bishops and most senior dignitaries of the Church were appointed, sometimes simoniacally, by the joint consent of king and pope. Rarely can the bishops of England have felt that responsibility for keeping the English people true to the Christian religion devolved upon them alone in council, while Rome continued to nominate and translate. Theologically, England looked to Europe (witness the initial enthusiasm expressed by the Church and the universities for the Council of Basel in 1432), for the frequently non-resident English bishops had little reputation as theologians. While Rome's ascendancy continued, there seemed no real cause for the bishops of England to act synodically or even theologically for the welfare of the English Church and people.[12]

The break with Rome brought about an entirely new situation. All authority in matters ecclesiastical, doctrine, discipline, property and finance now lay in the hands of king and Parliament. The king had entered into a new contract with the bishops. Corporately, in the Convocations, they had made an act of submission to the Royal Supremacy. Now they were to be granted the opportunity and endowed with the responsibility of guiding the church under the careful supervision and restraint of the state. The Convocations which before had met with little theological concerns on their agenda were by the time of the reign of Edward VI to be replete with questions of doctrine and liturgy. The Prayer Books, the Ordinal, the Articles, the Homilies, judgements on heretics, considerations of church order, morals, recusants and separatists – all were to be subjects for the conversation of bishops and the representative clergy of the Convocations of Canterbury and York. Never before in the history of the English Church had so much theological responsibility devolved upon the bishops of the English dioceses. True, nothing they resolved could become binding on the English people unless it had the force of law, which could only be given by Parliament. But Parliament was on the whole content to leave theology to the divines; whatever may be said about the secular authority being a godly lay voice, it was clergymen who drafted the new liturgy and clergymen who wrote the new theology. Symbolically, the Convocations met at the beginning of each new Parliament and were summoned by the king. They had to know their place. But with the Church's secular powers now firmly transferred to the Crown and with the absence of interference from Rome, it was safe to leave the Church's leaders to promote the new spiritual order within the restraints of the temporal authority.[13]

It is sometimes said that a biological organism which separates from its parent body has to assume the functions of the whole. If this is a fair analogy, it is true of the Church of England. The Council of Basel had failed an earlier generation – Archbishop Chichele had issued the summons for all who desired to attend. But within a year it was clear that that was not to be the forum for the much hoped-for ecclesiastical reform. In the reign of Elizabeth, with no opportunity for participation in the concluding sessions of the Council of Trent, the English bishops were committed as a body, isolated from the rest of Christendom, to their own tasks of government. Their task was one of continuity and reform; and predictably, as in the time of Theodore, they could not speak of reform without the assertion that the so-called 'new' religion was but a return to original apostolic and early Church purity. Their purpose, as Jewel said in his *Apology* was to 'shew it plain that God's holy gospel, the ancient bishops, and the primitive church do make on our side, and that we have not without just cause left these men, or rather have returned to the apostles and old catholic fathers'.[14] 'Who dare say that this is a new Religion', wrote Simon Patrick in 1687, 'which is as old as Christ and the Apostles?'[15] In this way, with its own councils and its historic title deeds, the catholic and apostolic Church in these islands searched the meaning of authentic Christianity.

It should not be imagined, however, that the Church of England now continued to order its affairs under the guidance and authority of its bishops with Parliament gently acceding to requests for necessary legislation. The Convocations, which were the only official forum for the bishops consisted not of bishops only but by their constitution included the house of the Lower Clergy, often vociferously opposed to the Upper House, eventually causing disagreements which led to the indefinite proroguing of both Convocations in 1742. Nor was Parliament on all occasions content to let the Convocations have their way. In 1710, William Whiston was accused of heresy by the Lower House of Convocation, found guilty by the Upper House and deprived of his post as Professor of Mathematics at Cambridge. He appealed to the Crown; and the opinion of the judges appointed to examine the case was that the Convocations might well try him but could not be regarded as the final court. In the event, they reserved judgement commenting, 'in case any records or proceedings which we are now strangers to shall be laid before us, or be suggested by the parties or their counsel to convince us of our mistakes', and Whiston went unharmed. Effectively the sovereign, not the bishops, had the last word.[16]

Two things were lacking, however, to the Church of England during the centuries following the Reformation. One probably went unnoticed or at least undefined until the middle of the nineteenth century and that was the need for a representative and predominantly episcopal council which would be allowed a freedom in debate and decision-making without the restrictions of the constitution which framed the Convocations. In 1850, Bishop Blomfield, then Bishop of London, commenting on the issue of Mr Gorham's denial of the doctrine of the baptismal regeneration of infants, said that nothing could be changed in the Church's traditional doctrine of baptism unless the formularies were 'altered by the authority of Convocation or of some synod equivalent to Convocation'. The Convocations, he continued, were not perfect and ought to be allowed freedom of speech and would speak with more weight if laymen were added to its counsels. 'I would not be understood', he concluded, 'to express an opinion unfavourable to the removal of those restrictions which hinder the Church from deliberating ... on doctrine and discipline.'[17] These were prophetic words. By 1886, his wish for the inclusion of the laity had become a reality; by 1919 the Convocations had been joined with an elected House of Laity to form the new National Assembly; and the General Synod today, though still under legal restraint, is clearly allowed that freedom of debate which Blomfield found so lacking in the Church of his own day. In this respect (though with some marked differences), the Church of England has moved in the direction of a theology which understands church councils as integral to the life of any province of the Christian Church.

The other lack was a severe absence of any communion or fellowship with the greater part of Christendom. Rome was viewed with suspicion, the Greek churches with respect and wonder (such as was known of them) but always with the sense that they, like Rome, had 'added' unnecessarily to the traditions of the primitive church. The provinces of Canterbury and York knew little of what it was to relate to provinces beyond the British Isles; and it is only with the growth of the Anglican Communion and the attempt in recent years to believe in this as a reality that the Church of England has discovered what it means to be part of a universal communion of churches. Ease of travel and swiftness of communication have brought the provinces of the Anglican Communion into far greater association than before was ever possible. And the need now felt for consultation, not only the sharing of local concerns but the mutual discussion of issues in faith and discipline, certainly calls for a new and international conciliar activity such as is germane to the very structures of the Church and integral to its life in the modern world. No longer at the Lambeth Conferences do colonial bishops come home to England; at Lambeth today, church meets church in the person of its bishop in the common pursuit of Christian truth and guidance for mission.

The Lambeth Conferences of the future are a great sign of hope both for ecumenism and for theology. To begin with, they are conferences of *bishops* and this is a characteristic which should be retained at all costs. At home, the bishops have the restraints of synods and governments; in conference at Lambeth they potentially exercise a traditional role of seeking to discern the mind of the Church and of formulating their own judgements on such aspects of Christain faith and living as are presented to them in the agenda under discussion. They are, in other words, free to exercise authority, not in the false sense that the bishops speak and the rest of the communion concurs, but in the sense that the bishops propose and the rest of the Church listens, judges and responds. No greater opportunity for progress in the exploration of Christian truth could be presented to the Anglican Communion. We have long needed our own Vatican Council; the Lambeth Conference as it stands is too limited in time to fulfil this requirement adequately, and past experience suggests that its agenda has not always been well conceived, while the debate has often focused more on ideology than theology. But the Conference still has all the potential for supplying an enormous need in the life of Anglicanism as a whole and should be reconsidered in this light.

The Lambeth Conference also offers hopes for reunion. For the Roman and Orthodox Communions to see Anglicans behaving synodically, with the bishops presiding and the clergy and laity fully consulted may well be of considerable reassurance. It is a pattern which both recognize. It is much easier to enter relationships with a Church which regards the 'synodal system' as a 'fundamental principle and essential characteristic'[18] of the Church then to negotiate with a Church which is reluctant to lose its national ties and the encumbrance of its faith in its peculiar history and culture. If this is clearly perceived, then the time should come when a representative synod of Anglican bishops meets with a similar synod of Roman or Orthodox bishops to debate the findings of the experts on the theological commissions and to confer on questions of pastoral and social concern. For the divided Christian churches to act unitedly in a synodical manner could well revive the memory that it was in this manner that the churches of antiquity rediscovered their essential unity.

Before this, however, the bishops of the Church of England need to rediscover their own synodical role in their own Church. At present they are restrained not only by Parliament but by the voting powers of the clergy and laity on the General Synod. It is true that they have a distinctive role in being empowered by the constitution of the General Synod to formulate proposals about change or reform in doctrine and worship; but should the clergy and laity oppose, or even one of the lower houses oppose, then the bishops are powerless to propose what they believe to be not only expedient but true to the rest of the Church of England. There is a great need at present for the bishops to be exposed to the whole range of feeling and opinion among the Christian populace at large. At the moment they are protected by the consideration that a firm proposition on their part in Synod may well be defeated in one or other of the lower houses. If it were a question (in matters of doctrine and discipline related to doctrine, e.g. the marriage discipline) of bishops having to face their own dioceses, their clergy and their laity and of presenting to them decisions which they believed they had made after full consultation, and if the bishops had to live with and take full responsibility for these decisions, then this might well condition their own debate within the House of Bishops. They have after all not only a seniority but a commission to the ministry of discernment.[19] This needs not only to be recognized but to be asserted; and the constitution of the General Synod stands in need of essential modification in this respect. The General Synod may undoubtedly debate doctrine and worship, in which process considerable pressure may be brought to bear on the bishops to follow the mind of the meeting.

But it would be to no discredit of the role of the clergy and the laity for the bishops to be allowed to make the final decisions and to invite the response from the rest of the Church. General Synods, like councils, may err; only time will tell whether the Synod has truly spoken in the name of Christ and under the guidance of the Spirit. But it is for the bishops with their unique relationship to their dioceses to take the first step and to bear the consequences on behalf of the clergy and people in their care.

The Church of England for all its curious history has never ceased to be an episcopal church. Episcopacy, as we have seen, is not purely a matter of pedigree, of having rightly ordained bishops appointed lawfully to appropriate episcopal sees. The bishop is very much a man of the people, drawn from them, representing them, serving them. He speaks their faith, and in so doing is the sign of their union with all other churches who profess that same faith. He is at the same time by his ordination and appointment a sign that their Church is continuous with and representative of the faith delivered by Christ to the apostles, that they are the authentic Christian community for their own locality and may genuinely promise the Christian message of life and hope to all among whom they live. It is he who must be allowed to speak through the councils of his fellow bishops. For it is he who by the consent of the people of God has been chosen for a unique ministry and in his office fulfils the ministry of the Good Shepherd. In hearing his voice we should hear our own voice; we are known of him, and he knows us. The episcopate is an office we should trust, for it is an office which sums up our own ministry – as Ignatius of Antioch said, the bishop in his own person *is* the multitude of the faithful.[20]

5 The Bishops and Ecumenism I – The Non-episcopal Churches

Proposals for reunion between the Church of England and the free or non-episcopal churches have been under discussion for more than sixty years. The Lambeth *Appeal to all Christian People* of 1920 reveals the serious intent of the bishops meeting at Lambeth in that year to work towards a united episcopally governed Church;[1] and the impetus given by Archbishop Fisher's Cambridge Sermon in 1947 resulted in the setting up in this country of official consultations between Anglicans and Methodists and Anglicans and Presbyterians. Abroad the successfully concluded South and North India unity schemes, though raising certain problems about reciprocal intercommunion with the Church of England, added considerably to the momentum for union between Anglicans and free churches in many parts of the world. At the same time, the post-war years have seen a burgeoning of episcopal/non-episcopal conversations, mostly in Europe and the United States which have provided a new dimension to problems once thought to be peculiarly British.[2] The meeting of Roman Catholics and French Protestants in the 'Groupe des Dombes',[3] for example, or the conversations between Roman Catholics and Lutherans in the United States have afforded insights which may well prove invaluable in helping to solve differences between the free and established churches of this country. So far, the Church of England has been significantly unsuccessful in promoting unity schemes with any branch of nonconformity. The Anglican–Methodist scheme, in progress since the late 1940s, failed to sustain the confidence of either Anglicans or Methodists and was abandoned in 1970. Then began 'Talks about Talks' involving all major Christian communions. This resulted in the setting up of the Churches Unity Commission which gave us the 'Ten Propositions'[4] and, eventually, firm proposals for covenanting between the churches.[5] In 1980 these proposals failed to secure a sufficient majority in their support and we have as yet no new, comparable scheme for church unity.

One of the questions that has bedevilled so many of these

discussions has been failure to reach agreement about the reconciliation of episcopal with non-episcopal ministries. Fisher in
1947 (in a famous phrase) urged the free churches to 'take
episcopacy into their system' or to 'try it out on their own ground'.
By and large there has been general agreement that whatever the
origins of episcopacy, the practice of having a chief pastor (called a
bishop), responsible for the clergy and people of one local church,
ordained by prayer with the laying on of hands, was at the lowest
estimate an appropriate pattern for a future united Church and at
highest the traditional pattern, discernible since apostolic times
and itself an outward sign of the Church's continuity in the
apostolic faith and with the apostolic ministry and mission.

If this were to be the case for the Church of the future, the
difficult question remains, what is to happen to existing Free
Church ministries if their churches are to reunite with the Anglican
Church. Some Anglicans would argue, 'Free Church ministers
have not been ordained by a bishop in the apostolic succession.
Therefore they need to be properly ordained.' Free Church ministers would reply, 'We have been appointed ministers of the word
and sacraments in our own churches; therefore the one thing we
do not require is ordination.'[6] Proposals have been made for
the mutual laying on of hands by Anglicans and Free Church
ministers alike. This, though the sentiments behind it are admirable, does give rise to the theory that there is something lacking in
each ministry and that somehow each needs to be 'topped up' (not
a very theological idea). The idea of reconciliation is better expressed in the 1980 Covenant Proposals in which all the clergy
involved say together, 'We seek God's blessing for the fulfilment
of our ministry' after which the presiding bishop prays for the
gift of the Holy Spirit on all present for their future ministry
together.[7] But this form has still failed to convince, and ministries
are not yet reconciled.

One of the fundamental weaknesses in all unity schemes since
the end of the Second World War has been an evident disjunction between the task of reconciling *churches* and that of reconciling *ministers*. It seems that the minute the ministerial problem
surfaces questions are asked about the minister: Who is he?
What can he do? Is he validly ordained?, etc., whereas the real
question is about churches. If, as we have shown at some length in
earlier chapters, the office of a bishop or priest or minister is

incomprehensible without reference to the church to which he has been appointed, then no reconciliation of ministries can be attempted without a firm proposal to unite all churches in a single communion, served by a single united ministry. In fairness, the Covenant Proposals of 1980 begin with the reconciliation of churches; but then there is a recess, after which the scheme continues to the reconciliation of existing ministers and the ordination of new ministers.[8] Somehow the two parts of such a scheme must become a single act.

We need, therefore, to return to what has been said earlier in this study about the bishop and the church. The bishop by definition is the one who has oversight and pastoral responsibility for one local church; but he is also in a real sense the embodiment of that church. In himself he represents its beliefs and convictions and is its foremost representative in the relation of that church to other churches. The episcopal office is not an organ of administration inserted into the body but an organism which grows within the body from the very beginning. Bishops are not gathered in some ecclesiastical Whitehall to be dispatched to govern and then return to their office of origin. When chosen and ordained, they become so much a part of the church which they serve that their office is meaningless without that church, just as the church cannot function truly as a church without the oversight of its chief minister. Our aim in ecumenical projects is to unite churches; but this cannot be done without in the same breath uniting ministries. There can be no disjunction between the declaration of the unity of churches and the declaration of the mutual acceptance and recognition of ministries. Somehow this has to be a combined exercise, though in reality it is a single act.

Let us look next at what is practically envisaged in the prospect of a united Church of the future. Some, understandably enough in the light of the many difficulties encountered, may be hoping at most for the freedom to attend church in whichever communion they choose and for a general interchange of ministries at altar and in pulpit. But this is to see only a part of the truth; the reality is that in a united Church, there will be only one Christian congregation in any one place, presided over by one minister, though he may be assisted by others and there may be several centres for meeting and worship. That is to say, if we are to plan realistically for the future, almost the first task is to adjust the map of dioceses and parishes, granting territorial responsibility to churches and chapels which at present have none so specified, removing all overlap in areas where Anglican and Free Churches coincide, creating more dioceses where needed, new parishes, new local areas of collegiality and co-operation (like the present Anglican deaneries and archdeaconries). This should have the effect of awakening in Christian people the sense that they are the people of God *in that place* and *for that place*, not Christians supporting a particular church or a particular chapel. Strict Congregationalists (particularly those who declined to join the United Reformed Church) would raise theological objections to this, and it has to be admitted that some Anglican congregations behave like Congregationalists in spending all their energies on propping up the church-going community with scant regard for the rest of the parish. But historic Christianity since New Testament times has always associated churches with places, not with congregations, even though some territorially organized churches, for example ECUSA, are essentially congregational in outlook. Churches overlapping in any one area have normally been seen as rivals rather than complementary.

If this is the first step in the design, then it involves two more decisions. First, it needs to be considered who are to be the chief pastors of the dioceses and second who are to have the oversight of the parishes. The first might be simply answered by recognizing the existing Anglican bishops as already exercising that responsibility. But there would undoubtedly be some new dioceses and there are already Free Church ministers who exercise the kind of oversight already held by Anglican diocesan bishops.[9] Whatever happens, each diocese should have no more than one bishop and where need arose, new bishops would have to be ordained. But where Free Church superintendents or presiding ministers serve an area which either overlaps with or is coterminous with an existing diocese, three possibilities arise. Either they should be made bishop of that diocese, and the existing Anglican bishop translated to another see, or they themselves should be moved to another diocese. Or for a time two chief pastors should remain responsible for the one diocese, one of them acting as coadjutor with right of succession should the other move, resign or die. This last is perfectly acceptable theologically and might well prove of great practical use in the early years of establishing the united Church.

At the parochial level, the problem seems more complex though the basic principles are the same as those affecting the episcopate. Each existing church or chapel should be designated to serve a particular area which would involve a redrawing of present Anglican parish boundaries – a not insuperable task, since this is regularly undertaken, e.g. in the uniting of benefices or reorganization of deaneries, although obviously very complicated if church and chapel are (as does happen) in close proximity to one another. To begin with this should in no way inhibit the Free Churches from continuing to draw from beyond their own area, a freedom which is enjoyed by most Anglican churches. It would mean, however, that on the one hand the Free Church minister would have a pastoral ministry beyond that of his immediate congregation (an understanding which many such ministers have today and exercise with some skill); and on the other hand that the rites of baptism, marriage and the burial of the dead would be customarily celebrated in the church of the area, whether formerly Anglican or nonconformist, liberty being allowed for individuals to choose not to go to their parish church if they prefer another place or another rite (another liberty which is common in Anglicanism). It is the principle here that counts; as there should be but one bishop to one diocese, so there should equally be one minister (sometimes with assistants) to one church in any one of the new areas or parishes.

The other tiers of administration (like the present Anglican deaneries and archdeaconries) would then become (as they are within Anglicanism) instruments of collegiality between ministers and therefore between churches. In some places, this is already being anticipated in clergy fraternals, local councils of churches and local ecumenical projects involving a number of local covenants. This is a useful preparation of the ground but is still exceptional and deserves recommendation and extension.

Having redrawn the map, we are now in a position to see churches rather than ministers and congregations – i.e churches of a place – served by the ministry of oversight, the ministers themselves being a collegial body representing their churches, whose unity is in turn served by the bishop of the diocese. But the question remains, How, if ever, could such a scheme be implemented? Who would agree to it? What are the objections?

First, any scheme of reunion between churches formerly separated implies as foundational to the whole exercise that the uniting churches share a common faith. In the recent proposals for the covenant (1980), for example, the covenanting churches renewed their baptismal promises and recited together the Nicene Creed.[10] Such a form is clearly a token of a wider reality. Although there are bound to be tensions in the sphere of doctrine and discipline which will require investigation and clarification (as was undertaken e.g. in the Anglican–Methodist Unity Commission Report of 1968) it seems likely that covenanting churches will recognize that there is a legitimate diversity of ethos and expression in teaching and worship, such as already exists *within* most communions at present.[11]

A further precondition is the commitment to work together in a united Church which, if it acknowledges what has already been said about the office of a bishop, will give the participating churches the sense that they join with the whole Church in the quest for Christian truth. For agreement in Christian doctrine is not simply a question of looking back to find a 'lowest common denominator' to which all may assent, but an exercise of creative theological thinking for the better expression of the faith in the twentieth century. And in this all would now be engaged, contributing insights that were lacking hitherto in any single communion.[12]

Second, with regard to the ministry. The phrase so often used in covenanting proposals, namely 'the mutual recognition of ministries', meaning that each minister of the churches seeking reunion recognizes ministers of other churches as true ministers of word and sacrament, needs to be replaced by a more creative and dynamic form of words. It is a phrase which by itself raises doubts in the minds of some Anglicans and is a primary stumbling-block for Roman Catholics. What is needed instead is a preliminary indication from the covenanting churches, which is agreed on by everyone, as to what vocation to the ordained ministry of the Church of God actually entails. This may take the form of an agreed Ordinal or of an agreed statement on ministry (or both).[13] But the churches must feel that they are moving into a new situation, not just patching up the past. They must admit their understanding of Christian ordained ministry in the past has been limited and is in need of reappraisal. In the proposal to undertake the task of ministry together, recent Ordinals and agreed statements have not only brought new insights for all concerned into the nature and vocation of the ordained ministry but have brought about a recognition that apparently different ordained ministries (e.g. Roman Catholic priest and Lutheran pastor) have the same character[14] and objectives. The same exploration should be undertaken (and perhaps these recent agreements used) to declare the identity in vocation and mission of all ministers of churches seeking reunion.

Next, one of the points that will inevitably emerge from any agreed statement about ministry is that though the minister is selected from the church and approved by the church, his vocation is from Christ through the church and this vocation is confirmed and authorized by the laying on of hands with prayer by the bishop, the church's chief pastor in that place. If it is thought that there might be considerable Free Church objection to such a theology, then it should be remembered that French Protestantism, in the shape of members of an ecumenical group called the 'Groupe des Dombes', was perfectly happy to accept the fact that the laying on of hands with prayer by the bishop was the 'normal sign' of appointment to ministerial office;[15] and in the Anglican–Methodist conversations, it was considered integral.[16] The absence of such a sign in Free Church ordinations or the fact that Free Church ordinations are not by someone called a bishop does not say anything detrimental about the efficacy of Free Church ministries. We are here not talking about quality or effectiveness, but of unity and collegiality and of a common authorization.

This being agreed, it must now finally be asked what course of action is appropriate. The task is basically to unite churches and, as we have said, is inseparable from that of reconciling ministers. The very act of reconciling ministers who have the oversight of churches is in itself a sign of the reunion of churches, but it must be understood in this light and not as a means of 'validating' ministries that before were in doubt. That the consequences of such an act will result in free access to communion of one Church with another shows that the earlier emphasis on 'validity' was theologically at heart a concern about communion and fellowship and not solely about what the minister 'was' or what the minister 'could do'.

It would seem therefore that the central feature of any act of union must be the appointment of ministers. Reunion and covenanting schemes hitherto have concentrated very heavily on this for good reason. This being so then, the process of reunion must begin at the provincial level, the metropolitans' (and new metropolitans') first concern being with the new dioceses and in some cases with the appointment of new chief pastors from the ministry of the Free Churches who henceforward will be called bishops.

Exactly the same process can then be echoed at the level of the diocese. In this case, the bishop of the diocese will be concerned with new parishes and the appointment of ministers to serve these new parishes. At each level, there will then be created a wider episcopal collegiality with the metropolitan and of an extended presbyteral council with the diocesan. But the collegiality, as has been shown earlier, is not the creation of a clerical club or a distancing of ministers into an exclusive hierarchy, but in itself is the very sign, traditional to historic Christianity, of the fellowship of *churches* with one another and of their search for a proper faithfulness to the gospel in the modern world.

Even so, how is such a step to be taken? First, the bishop or metropolitan in any act of reconciliation must declare that the ministers of Free Churches have, like their colleagues who have been episcopally ordained, already received the gift of God appropriate to the fulfilment of their ministry. This was prayed for at their ordination and undoubtedly received. This being so, a joint renewal of ordination vows might well be one of the preliminaries to the act of reconciliation itself.

Second, the bishop must perform a deliberate act of reconciliation and fellowship towards those who formerly were not part of his presbyteral council, just as the metropolitan will have to do the same towards those in the Free Churches exercising comparable oversight to that of a diocesan bishop and now to be bishops of the new dioceses. Here the laying on of hands with prayer would seem the only possible rite. To those who fear that such an act would imply 'reordination' it should be made clear that hands are laid on with prayer for many purposes (healing, confirmation, reconciliation of penitents, etc.) and that it is the form (i.e. the words used) that indicates the intention and purpose of the rite.

One form has already been proposed (in *Growing into Unity*), though so far it has not gained any wide acceptance. The text reads: 'I, A. B., Bishop of . . . in the United Church, do recognize and accept you as a Presbyter in the Church of God, now to serve within the Presbyterate of this Diocese in the three-fold ministry of this Church. I now commit to you authority to exercise your ministry within this Church wherever you may be called and licensed. May God use your ministry to His greater glory.'[17]

The main difficulty with this is that it does not say anything about the *place* where the presbyter is to serve or the *church* which he is already serving. It treats him at face value, rather like a *presbyter vagans* needing to be regularized, a man looking for a job, a minister of a congregation without roots. It also seems to concentrate too much on the juridical aspect of the relationship between bishop and presbyter rather than the theological relationship of the bishop, through the presbyter, to the total pastoral ministry of any one place. So another form is needed.

Remembering that in this particular proposed act of reconciliation, the bishop is speaking to ministers of Free Churches who are to assume full pastoral responsibility for the entire population of an area from which hitherto they have only drawn those of their own denomination, an appropriate form of words might be as follows: 'I, A. B., Archbishop/Bishop and chief pastor of the Province/Diocese of . . . do first welcome you as a minister of the Church of God into the episcopal/presbyteral fellowship of this Province/Diocese, praying that God may forgive the sins and offences which have formerly separated us, and grant us grace to serve Him in unity and concord. And by the authority given unto me by Our Lord Jesus Christ in the Church, I hereby authorize you to have the pastoral care and oversight of the Diocese/Parish of X . . . which is your care and mine. May God grant you his grace to fulfil this service to His greater glory.'

The advantages of such a form are several. It is quite specific in what is declared, it applies to the individual, recognizing him for what he believes himself to be, yet extending his ministry in the embrace of a wider fellowship. To those who object that there is nothing said about the minister so commissioned being a priest, it may be pointed out that (a) the rite is that of the laying on of hands with prayer by the bishop (the 'normal sign' of fellowship in apostolic faith and mission) and that (b) the bishop is acknowledging that the minister is to undertake the same pastoral care and oversight in the parish that he (the bishop) exercises in the diocese – 'your care and mine'. There is a unity, that is to say between the bishop's ministry and that of the Free Church ministers, so commissioned; and their common understanding of ministry as set out in the new ordinals or agreed statements on ministry will already have been researched and the priestly aspect of this ministry commonly understood.

Should the Free Church ministers in turn lay hands on their Anglican colleagues? This has been suggested in both the Anglican–Methodist proposals and in the report *The Reconciliation of Ministries* (GS 307). The difficulty here is that if the rite of laying on of hands with prayer in this context is seen as expressly connected with the setting up of new parishes and *not* with the regularization of ministers formerly regarded as irregular, then there is no need for any more laying on of hands by anyone to be done. If it were, then it would lead us back into the jungle, either persuading us that all ministries were insufficient and in need of 'topping up' or that Anglican clergy were being admitted to minister to *congregations* of Free Church members rather than to the ministry of the *Church* in any one *place*.

Is this form equally sufficient for the appointment of new bishops from among the senior ministers of the Free Churches? It would seem so, if it is remembered that the principle underlying each appointment is exactly the same. A Methodist superintendent minister, for example, who by common agreement is appointed bishop of one of the new dioceses will receive (a) an acknowledgement that he already exercises an episcopal ministry and (b) a commissioning to exercise that ministry in a particular diocese.

What has been said above may leave the reader with the sense that he has travelled to Utopia where the inhabitants always behave in a reasonable and logical way. Knowing the legal and personal difficulties that already complicate life in the Church, the exercise of reuniting Anglican and Free Churches by any means is never going to be straightforward. But this has been written, with acknowledgement to many earlier studies, in this conviction that episcopacy and church are inseparable, just as church and geographical location can never properly be divided. Bishop, church, place; presbyter, church, place – such is the traditional pattern of Christian ministry and the only practicable structure for the united Church of the future.

6 The Bishops and Ecumenism II – The Roman Catholic Church

Any schemes for Church unity in this country must at the out-set take into account the fact that of the 3.5 million practising Christians resident in England, more than one half are Roman Catholics. It has sometimes been naively thought that since re-union with Rome is a rather distant prospect, the restoration of communion between the Church of England and those who separated from her over the past four centuries should come first as the problems do not seem quite so intractable and as there is the common bond between them of the Reformed tradition. Despite considerable advances, this has not proved to be the case; and if one of the main purposes of Christian unity is to unite the Church's mission, then it is imperative that the two numerically strongest communions – the Roman Catholic and the Anglican – should if anything lead the way.

The setting up of the Anglican–Roman Catholic International Commission in 1969 has, as is well known, resulted in theological agreement being reached by the Commission in three areas – those of the Eucharist, the ministry and authority. The final report was published in January 1982[1] and in the concluding pages, the authors remind readers that 'This dialogue ... has been directed not merely to the achievement of doctrinal agreement, which is central to our reconciliation, but to the far greater goal of organic unity. The convergence reflected in our Final Report would appear to call for the establishing of a new relationship between our Churches as a next stage in the journey towards Christian unity.'[2] Earlier (in 1976) at the conclusion of the first statement on authority, the commission had expressed this sentiment even more sharply: 'we submit our Statements to our respective auth-orities', they write, 'to consider whether or not they are judged to express on these central subjects a unity at the level of faith which not only justifies but *requires action* to bring about a closer sharing between our two communions in life, worship, and mission.' (My italics.)[3] The move, in other words, is for practical steps to be taken in order to demonstrate that agreement on issues which seemed to divide leads logically to a new relationship between the churches.

It might well be thought that a major stumbling-block in any practical scheme for reunion would be the fact that in 1896, the Roman Catholic Church declared Anglican ordinations to be 'absolutely null and utterly void'. Roman Catholics have never officially looked upon Anglican clergy as fully authorized ministers of word and sacrament; none could say publicly that Anglican ministries 'have been manifestly blessed and owned by the Holy Spirit as effective means of grace' (as the Lambeth Conference of 1920 stated about Free Church ministries). And though today there are many in the Roman Communion who have not the slightest qualms about seeing Anglican clergy and their congregations as genuine and effective partners in mission, there can at present be no question of a 'mutual recognition of ministries' such as was suggested in the *Covenant Proposals* of 1980.[4] It is true that the Anglican–Roman Catholic International Commission did say that the question of Anglican ordinations could now be looked at afresh in the new context of 'agreement on the essentials of eucharistic faith with regard to the sacramental presence of Christ and the sacrificial dimension of the eucharist and on the nature and purpose of priesthood, ordination and apostolic succession'.[5] The Catholic Truth Society has included a new publication, *Anglican Orders – A Way Forward?* (by E. J. Yarnold) to accompany its standard pamphlet, *Are They Priests? The Nature of Anglican Orders* (by Maurice Bévenot). But the fascinating debate about the judgement of Leo XIII in the Bull, *Apostolicae Curae* (probably one of the best games of ecclesiastical chess this century) has not resulted in either side conceding victory.

This however is not the real *impasse*. Narrow views of ministry and ordination have led some Roman Catholics to believe that since Anglican clergy are not true priests, the sacraments which they celebrate are not true means of grace. Roman Catholics receive the true Body and Blood of Christ; Anglicans receive bread and wine, and any grace that God chooses to give through their ministrations is purely uncovenanted. Crude though this interpretation may seem, it has in the past, certainly, been widespread.[6] But as we have seen, ordination in the Christian Church is not simply a question of the conferring of power to perform certain functions, but of authority to proclaim the apostolic faith and to be trusted with the leadership and oversight of a local apostolic Church. Many an Anglican priest could claim that his 'pedigree' gives him powers identical to those of any Roman Catholic priest (through the participation of Old Catholic bishops in the consecration of his ordaining bishop) which under the narrower view of ordination we have outlined would be hard to deny. But a fully comprehensive Catholic view of ordination would show very clearly that despite such a succession, the Anglican clergy remain separated from the communion of the universal Church, centred on the see of Rome, and therefore lack the authority to exercise their ministry. In the Roman Catholic view, the authority of a bishop, though given him directly by Christ at his ordination, can only be exercised in communion with his fellow bishops and with the Bishop of Rome; and the authority of a parish priest is delegated to him directly by his bishop and can similarly only be exercised within the jurisdiction of his diocesan bishop or by special permission from another diocesan should the occasion arise.

If anything, therefore, the question of authority looms considerably larger than the question of validity in the reconciliation of Anglican and Roman Catholic ministries and churches. When the time for reunion comes, the validity of Anglican ordinations will have to be very carefully re-examined in the light of the 'new context'. But both communions in their rites of ordination, as well as in their respective compilations of Canon Law, never envisage an ordained ministry being exercised without the requisite authority of a bishop or outside the communion of the Church to which the minister belongs. The Anglican Communion, for example, has made its position absolutely clear about those ordained by the so-called *episcopi vagantes*.[7] A bishop, however validly consecrated, who is out of communion with the rest of the Anglican episcopate cannot expect priests ordained by him to be admitted into the ministerial work of the Anglican Church. In this judgement they echo the fundamental theology in this matter of the Roman Catholic Communion. Ordination is a commission given by Christ in and for the Church. Those so commissioned are first and foremost men under authority and men committed to a fellowship.[8] It is disregard for authority and separation from the fellowship which is the primary cause of a ministry ceasing to be trustworthy and becoming potentially fruitless. The question of pedigree, though by no means unimportant, always remains secondary to these considerations.

Supposing, however, that the 'new context' in which Anglican ordinations are now to be considered does eventually lead to the view (on the part of the Roman Catholic Church) that the churches of the Anglican Communion, though separated, are nonetheless 'churches' – genuine manifestations of the mystery of God's redeeming work in Christ with an effective ordained ministry under whose care and guidance men and women find their way to God. This is a view which many Roman Catholics already hold (albeit unofficially). The generous, for example, will say, 'I am sure God blesses the ministry of our local Anglican clergyman and that his people receive grace through the sacraments which he celebrates.' But a more astute theological critique will suggest that, kindly and sincerely though this may be meant, it doesn't touch the real issue. What some Roman Catholic theology will ask is, 'How can a Church or communion of churches that has lived in separation from the rest of Christendom for over four hundred years remain true to the catholic and apostolic faith when it has broken from that communion which to our mind is the essential safeguard of Christian truth?'[9] This is a very basic question and must be looked at with some care.

From the very beginning of the Christian era, unity has been a fundamental mark of the Church. 'The Church which fills the whole world', wrote St Irenaeus of Lyons (d. AD 220), 'and which guards securely the traditions of the Apostles, offers to all but a single faith. All confess their faith in the same God, all believe in the same economy of salvation by the Incarnation of the Son of God, and in recognition of the identical gifts they have received from the one Spirit, endeavour to follow the same precepts. The same form of organization is preserved amongst them, and all are looking for the same Coming of the Lord, and earning a salvation which is the same for all men' (*Adv. Haer.* III.2.1.). So much is this so that for St Irenaeus it can be safely said that where there is not this same faith, there is no Church. Heretical and schismatic bodies may proclaim Christian allegiance as much as they will. But (as he says later in the same book)[10] if they argue against the apostolic churches, they are attempting to refute the apostles themselves whose successors now preside in their place and who preserve the tradition that was committed to them. A break from the fellowship of the apostolic churches means a break with Christianity. No compromise can be admitted.

Nearly two hundred years later, Augustine of Hippo was to echo the same theme. The situation which he faced in North Africa was not entirely unlike our own in this country and has often been appealed to by way of illustration (not always, may it be said, with success). Augustine inherited a situation whereby the Catholic Church which claimed to be the authentic apostolic Church of the province had to live side by side with the Donatist Church, which claimed to be the only representative of true Christianity since only the Donatists had kept the faith in time of persecution. In every town and village therefore, there was a Catholic and a Donatist church; to every diocese, there was a Catholic and Donatist bishop. The Catholics never for once questioned the validity of Donatist orders, nor even (so far as Augustine was concerned) of Donatist sacraments. Donatists on the other hand considered all Catholic sacraments and ministries invalid, doubted whether Catholics could be called Christian at all, and in some quarters mounted an offensive against Catholic Christians by way of regular acts of violence and rebellion. Neither the Catholic Church nor the civil government can be seen as entirely blameless in this episode. But the two Churches claiming to teach the same faith and being structured in exactly the same way, were rivals. The challenge was to make them partners.[11]

Augustine's main complaint against the Donatists was that they had separated from unity and in doing so had trampled on the law of charity. The sacraments, he rightly claimed, were 'incarnate charity'.[12] Nobody, for example, ought to receive the sacrament of the altar in his parish church on Sunday if he were seriously at odds with his family or neighbours during the week. You cannot come to receive love incarnate with hatred in your heart. How much less can a Donatist Christian who hates not only the Catholics in North Africa but takes a dim view of Christians in every other country in the world, celebrate or even receive the sacrament of reconciliation and love? By these criteria even baptism comes unstuck. Baptism is into the one Body of Christ, it is (as F. D. Maurice was to say many years later) the sign of our union with Christ and our fellowship with one another. Donatists baptized in order to separate people, just as they stood at a Donatist altar in order to raise the flag against the Catholics. The whole thing was a nonsense; and therefore Augustine judged that Donatist sacraments were indeed valid, but administered in such total uncharity they could not possibly be regarded as doing any good – in his words, they were 'inefficacious'.

The cure for this lay partly with the theologians (and here the Donatists had some of the most eminent of their day), and partly with those within whose powers it lay to bring an end to civil disorder. The ability to inspire the will to move from a state of competition to contemplating what it would be like to work together is certainly one of Augustine's major achievements. To this end, as is well known, he involved both the Church and the state. But the final solution, when it came (at the Conference of Carthage in 411) was based partly on the large measure of theological agreement that had been reached but principally on a firm decision to become partners in mission and to share all the resources available. No one was ousted (apart from the few who refused to accept the agreement). Donatist bishops stayed in their sees, shared with the Catholic bishop in the work of oversight, succeeded to him as sole bishop if he died. Nobody was rebaptized, nobody was reordained. With unity now restored, Augustine could see no objection to either Donatist ministries or sacraments. The sacraments were now administered in unity and in charity. Immediately, they became efficacious.

For both Irenaeus and Augustine, therefore, unity – being in communion with the catholic and apostolic Church – is of the essence of being a Christian. The same holds good for the modern Roman Catholic Church. Though obviously (particularly in the light of the Second Vatican Council) no Roman Catholic would call members of other denominations 'non-Christian', the fullness of Christian life is still officially to be found within the unity of the Roman Catholic Communion.[13] This makes it very difficult for Roman Catholics to understand a church which at the local and provincial level has preserved the same form of church order and ministry, which reads the same Scriptures, recites the same creeds, celebrates what at least appear to be the same sacraments, teaches very similar precepts and claims to be an authentic part of the one holy catholic and apostolic Church. It is all the more difficult since ecumenical dialogues all over the world have shown that traditional differences between Anglicans and Roman Catholics are by no means so deep-rooted as they first appeared and that there is far more identity at the level of faith between the two churches than had been thought even twenty years ago. Despite the evident difference in culture and custom, theological language and discipline, an informed Roman Catholic today might well be tempted to say that the churches of the Anglican Communion have preserved and grown in the catholic and apostolic faith in an individual but nonetheless authentic way, and therefore deserve to be regarded as churches in the fullest sense, save that they do not share in that essential unity offered and enjoyed by the churches in communion with the see of Rome.[14]

The more pessimistic, however, may rightly ask, How is it possible for a Church to grow in this way when it has so blatantly rejected (and been rejected by) the wider communion of churches in whose councils it ought to have shared in the common exploration of Christian truth? Here Cyprian of Carthage, a great architect of church unity who had no time for those who withdrew from episcopal fellowship, may nonetheless be of help. His book *On the Unity of the Catholic Church*,[15] written in the mid-third century, probably had in mind a schism at Rome (caused by a rigorist sect which split off in the wake of the Decian persecution and appointed its own bishop, Novatian) and in its second recension may have taken into account disagreements between himself and the pope, Stephen, about the rebaptism of those baptized in schism. For Cyprian, like most of the Fathers, unity is a mark of the Catholic Church; to him every separated Church, every isolated bishop is anathema. But his real question is, What do we mean when we say that there is only one Church? And the answer is that the unity of the Church lies in its *origins*. In the beginning, says Cyprian, the Church was one; and from this single origin it has spread like a stream from its source, like a tree from its root, like the many rays from the single sun until it is now dispersed throughout the entire world. Like the seamless robe of Christ, the Church has been woven from the top to the bottom, from its origins at its foundations to the broad hem which now envelops the earth. Casting on the first stitches was the secret and cause of its seamlessness. He gives another example. In the Gospel of St Matthew it is recorded that the Lord willed to found the Church on Peter, '... you are Peter, and on this rock I will build my church' (Matt. 16.18). The Church was therefore founded on one man, not on twelve. For although the other apostles were 'all that Peter was' nevertheless a 'primacy was given to Peter' in order to demonstrate that the Church had its origins in unity. It began, so to speak from one man, so that being founded *supra unum* and beginning from one (*initium* and *fundamentum* are synonymous terms here), it might effectively be caused to remain one and always be recognized as one. *Exordium ab unitate proficiscitur*, he writes, *ut ecclesia Christi una monstretur* (it has its origins in unity in order that the Church of Christ may be shown to be one).[16]

This being the case, it can be clearly shown that the catholic and apostolic churches, scattered throughout the world, share a common unity not least because they share a common origin. This does not of course abrogate the need for outward signs of collegiality between church leaders and for conciliar activity on the part of all the churches. But it does strongly underpin a theology of the Church which declares (as we have seen) every local church to be a church in its own right by reason of its apostolic origins, a full and complete manifestation of the totality of God's saving mystery in Christ; and it does support a theology of the episcopate which declares a bishop to have received his authority not mediately (as it might be from the pope) but directly from Christ through the church which appoints him. 'There is only one episcopal office', writes St Cyprian, in which every bishop shares, but he holds the office 'in totality'.[17] The 'episcopate' for Cyprian, is never a collective term. Each bishop is bishop in his own right, as each church is a church in its own right. Bishop and church together go back to a common root; and it is this root and source which is the dynamic cause of present unity.[18]

Comparing modern ecumenical situations with those of the patristic era has its hazards and is considered by some to be positively dangerous. Nonetheless, the three patristic sources we have quoted may shed some light on the present situation of Anglicans and Roman Catholics.

First, St Irenaeus with his emphasis on 'the same faith'. The aim of all Anglican–Roman Catholic dialogue is to discover agreement in matters of faith, particularly in those areas of doctrine where division seemed most apparent. Agreed statements, both in this country and abroad, have shown that there is remarkable potential in such an exercise and the hope is that eventually, allowing for differences in culture and theological language, both sides will be able to assert together that they are in full agreement on what it means to believe and practice as a Christian.

Second, St Augustine with his emphasis on unity and charity. There can be no doubt that historical processes have brought about an immense change in the attitude of Anglicans and Roman Catholics towards one another in this country. After the long years of disability, Roman Catholics today suffer no disadvantages for their religious allegiance (the monarchy being virtually the only office at present closed to them) and attitudes have changed so remarkably that in many countries (sadly not all) the majority in both churches look upon one another as fellow Christians with a common cause. Vestiges of competition remain, for the folk memory is long, but there are signs (such as the hundred or more local ecumenical projects in this country) that many more than before are looking for partnership. Traditional hostilities are more or less a thing of the past; charity has been restored. What many are looking for is both the means and the authority to make partnership not only possible but effective.

Cyprian would no doubt have been horrified by the existing state of affairs in the Western Church. 'Disunion', he wrote, 'can never lead to the Kingdom of God ... Those who have refused to be of one mind in the church of God cannot therefore be abiding in God.'[19] He was not of course a European, he did not live through the Reformation and the Enlightenment and belonged to a world over which a single civilization had established a remarkable unity. He did on the other hand see the federation of the Christian Church of his own day as a *consequence* of their common origins and subsequent identity, and he did see the collegiality of the bishops as resulting from the share of each in totality in the one episcopal office. If an individual local Church were to enjoy unity with the rest, it was certainly due in part to the fact that it had remained true to its origins and retained its identity as being fully catholic and apostolic (for the terms 'catholic' and 'apostolic' were applied in the first instance to the local church and not to the universal Church), as St Ignatius of Antioch is the first to make clear.[20] Once a Church is established – not a sect or a philanthropic society, but a *Church* – founded by the authority which comes through a duly authorized episcopate and the fellowship of the universal communion of churches and a form of life and belief which is unquestionably Christian, then there is a dynamic of unity which flows through such a Church from its origins to the present. Such a Church is naturally endowed with the capacity for collegial life with all other churches. The potential for unity is within itself;[21] making that unity real through collegial activity with the rest of Christendom is a first priority.

Should, however, a group of churches separate – as the Church of England did in the sixteenth century – and embark on a course of life independent from the greater part of Christendom, it should never be said that theologically, the separated churches are a 'branch' of the one catholic Church which happens to be travelling in its own direction. Defenders of the so-called 'branch theory' of the Church would say that the separated communion comes from the same tree, has the same origins, the same roots and produces the same kind of foliage and fruit. And there may be some who would invoke St Cyprian as supporting this theology, just as they would incorrectly quote St Augustine as saying that there are valid sacraments outside the Catholic Church. But such a theology represents neither Cyprian nor Augustine nor the gospel itself. A Church determined to continue in disunity, according to these, is committing an unpardonable sin; only when it turns to rediscover a unity which is inherent in its charter will the damage begin to be repaired.

Modern historians, in their judgements on the schisms of the sixteenth century, are fortunately far less prone to exalt either the Roman or the Anglican Church into the position of either hero or villain of the piece than those of an earlier generation. The sheer complexity of the issues – political, social and theological – makes that kind of analysis virtually impossible. Most of us look back in sadness at the positive evil that was done by so many to so many, but with thankfulness for the creative insights which emerged through that amazing era of growth and discovery. In short, 'Who left who?' is a question that seems to have a simple answer; but given the circumstances, it would be hard to say that the Church of England struck out on its own course for purely selfish motives and without any sense that in its reforms it was contributing to the greater good of Christendom as a whole (as its links at the time with much Continental Christianity would indicate). What matters today, however, is that both churches are now actively seeking reunion with one another and preparing for partnership. In theology and worship many apparent differences are beginning to be resolved and the practical side of a joint church life is already being explored. There has been an undoubted change of heart on the part of both churches at all levels; they can no longer be looked upon as rivals, even though deep fears still remain to be overcome in both communions. The main thing is that the will for unity is there. Cyprian and Augustine would never tolerate two churches defying one another, each claiming to be representing authentic Christianity. But they would have a lot of compassion for two churches planning a future unity, and would furthermore believe this a real possibility.

One question remains. Can the Roman Communion only look upon Anglicans as a group of Christians (and some of them very remarkable Christians) who probably through no fault of their own have, so to speak, 'fallen out of the basket', been sustained in their communities by the grace of God and now need to be reintegrated into catholic unity? Or can it in all truthfulness see Anglicanism as a communion of *churches* with structures at the local level identical to its own and a faith which as time goes on appears to them more and more the same in its essentials as that which they themselves profess? Is it, in other words, sufficient for Roman Catholics in their ecumenical enquiry to begin to say, 'Yes, Anglicans are Christians and believe much of what we do. Please respect them accordingly and work with them when you can'? Or is the Roman Church now prepared to meet Anglicanism in its structures, not merely in its theologians?[22] Can bishop meet bishop as bishop? Can a synod of Anglican bishops meet in council with a synod of Roman Catholic bishops? Is this the ecumenism of the future?

There are obviously going to be doubts and reservations on the Roman Catholic side if the requirement should be made that any Roman bishop attending a joint synod of Roman and Anglican bishops had to acknowledge publicly his Anglican colleague as an equal in office and order. Purple all round the table will not allay theological fears; but the sheer fact of being round the table may. Augustine must have had many worries about the Donatist bishops. The behaviour of some within living memory had been frankly bizarre and the selection and education of others left much to be desired. But none of this deterred him from urging a full consultation with all present, once he felt that the theological differences were beginning to be resolved. History, in other words, suggests that a direct encounter in conference is a better risk than a grudgng acknowledgement in the street. There may be doubts in the Roman mind about Anglican bishops, their beliefs, their role and their authority; but with many theological differences now so fully explored, to meet in synod as men with the care of the churches as their chief concern and with what may emerge as a remarkably common mind about their own role in such care could greatly further the cause of Christian unity.

It is for this reason that the bishops of the Anglican Communion should value their own right to meet synodically. As a worldwide communion of churches, Anglicanism has a remarkable opportunity to demonstrate its concern for its own internal unity through its representatives, the bishops. Though a necessary administrative tier such as the Anglican Consultative Council may serve to promote this unity, it is primates' conferences, Lambeth Conferences and any other form of episcopal synod that will lend the necessary credibility to this exercise in the eyes of the Roman and Orthodox churches which are firmly committed to the synodal system. It is equally important too (as we have seen in chapter four) for the bishops of the Church of England to reassure the rest of Christendom that they also bear the heavy responsibility of discerning the mind of the Church, of speaking that mind and of listening to and assessing the response of the Christian public. The present constitution of the General Synod stands in need of careful amendment in order to allow this distinctive and central role of the bishops to be clearly understood. The gains in so doing, particularly in the ecumenical sphere, will be far larger than the losses that may be feared.

Nothing has been said so far about the papacy. Popes, as is well known, are not consecrated or ordained to a new order, but elected and enthroned. The quintessence of the papal office is the fact that the pope is a bishop; the uniqueness of it is that he is Bishop of Rome. His papal office is basically his episcopate 'writ large', extending his pastoral concern to the whole of the Roman Catholic Communion, as the primate of a province serves the needs of all the dioceses in his area – without of course detracting from the authority of diocesan bishops. Anglicans will from time to time wonder at the strange and sometimes threatening language used of the pope's authority, his immediate, ordinary and universal jurisdiction, his infallibility, and the fact that he is pope 'by divine right'.[23] They may have reservations too about seeking reunion with a Church in which decisions made at a great height seem to become uncomfortably binding on those with little chance of seeking redress. But twenty years have seen much change, conquest of prejudice and new understanding. There is undoubtedly more to come. All are asking questions about primacy, which all episcopal churches encounter. In the Anglican view, the universal primacy of the pope may seem too weighty; yet in their own communion, primates carry heavy responsibility with limited authority which may for their purposes be too light. But should the Church of the future find that unity is best served through the office of a universal primate, then it will be on the assurance that that office is essentially episcopal, is exercised in collegiality and speaks not the mind of one man and his advisers but of all the churches of Christendom. Theologically speaking, this is true of the papacy today. We can only pray that an office so exercised may become acceptable, basically because it is a recognizably true expression of episcopacy.

Excursus I – The Origins of the Episcopate

The subject of Christian origins is dangerous ground. Today, any attempt to describe the development of the ordained ministry is bound to be greeted with qualifications, and charges of mythologizing upon the limited evidence in order, it will be said, to prove that a certain structure is original to the Church and therefore God's will for the future. The study of Christian origins has other purposes however, not least of which is to gain some insight into the character and purpose of the ordained ministry and therefore to see new perspectives in that ministry as it is exercised today. What follows may therefore not always find favour with the scholarly critic; but elements in it may nonetheless be found illuminating for our contemporary situation.

It is tempting to begin the study of the origins of the ordained ministry with a consideration of the titles given to those who held office in the primitive Christian communities as bishops, presbyters and deacons. It is immediately evident, however, that this is not the 'threefold' ministry as we know it today. To begin with, there is more than one bishop at Philippi (Phil. 1.1) as well as a group of elders/presbyters at Miletus (Acts 20.17) and there seems to be no difference in rank between them. By the end of the first century, however, the picture is changing. The Pastoral Epistles, the first epistle of St Clement of Rome and the letters of Ignatius of Antioch reveal the emergence of a situation in which churches are headed by a chief minister called a bishop, while the title presbyter refers to members of a collegiate body of clergy who (in Syria at least) assist the bishop.[1] The diaconate remains virtually unaltered, though it is considered a ministry of considerable dignity, the 'type' of the deacon, according to Ignatius, being Christ himself whereas the presbyters in their collegiality are best typified by the society of the apostles.[2]

The question is then asked, 'What happened?' Through a dark tunnel, the churches have changed from being communities governed by what seems to be a council of several to societies subjected to a strict hierarchy which Christians ignore at their peril.[3] The bishop is now monarch and every kind of abuse of ecclesiastical power which has brought misery to the Church in many ages is seen in embryo in this new situation. Small wonder that the episcopate has loomed large in the assaults of the Reformers, and that alternative forms of church government have been proposed which are believed to be far closer to the intentions of Christ as revealed to the apostles.[4]

We could say (with Liberal Protestantism) that this development is an early sign of the church 'hardening' and losing its first spontaneity. Institution seems to take over where inspiration begins to fail, and subsequent history has shown the inevitable conflict between the hardened hierarchy of the priests and the charismatic fervour of the prophets.

We could on the other hand say that this was indeed a development but a development in the right direction. If that is the case, then the new situation must have preserved and expressed certain principles about the gospel and its transmission already worked out in the structures of the earliest Christian communities; and that therefore there must be a basic continuity between the ministries described in the New Testament and those evidenced in the sub-apostolic Church. The challenge then is to describe this continuity.

One approach to the subject is to look at such evidence as we have for the rite of ordination. In the apostolic age it would appear that certain ministers were appointed to office (at least in some places) by the act of laying on of hands with prayer. Though the rite has parallels in the earlier history of Judaism and in first-century Rabbinic practice (Rabbis being ordained by their teachers after the manner of Joshua who was 'ordained' by Moses – Num. 27; Deut. 31)[5] the New Testament texts must in the first instance be examined in their immediate context. Acts 6.6 refers to the commissioning of the Seven (sometimes called deacons but never actually named as such); Acts 13.1–3 to the sending out of Paul and Barnabas on their mission; Acts 14.23 to the ordination of elders at Miletus (though the term for ordination here is *cheirotonia* and could simply mean 'election');[6] 1 Tim. 4.14, taken together with 2 Tim. 1.6, to the laying on of hands on Timothy by Paul ('with the presbytery') and 1 Tim. 5.22, in which Timothy is warned to 'lay hands suddenly on no man' to Timothy's commissioning role. Apart from the references in the

Pastoral Epistles, the occasions described are all very different and it would be rash to make any generalizations at this stage.

What is beginning to emerge, however, is a basic principle, namely that positions of responsibility and leadership in the early Christian communities were not filled simply by election, but those holding them required authorization or commission. Stephen in Acts 6 is, after all, chosen for his suitability by the people as are Barnabas and Saul (by the community at prayer, Acts 13.2), but it is the commissioning by the laying on of hands which marks the beginning of their new work, as it is this which is the authorization for their task. According to the fourth evangelist, the apostles themselves understood their own ministry in this light; as Jesus' ministry would have been deprived of its central purpose had he not believed that he had been sent by the Father (John 20.21, 'As the Father has sent me', cf. Heb. 3.1, 'Jesus, the apostle and high priest') so the apostles understood themselves to have been not only selected by Christ (John 15.16, 'I chose you') but also commissioned by him (John 20.21, 'even so I send you'). It is understandable, therefore, that a pattern of commissioning should have emerged as the expression and outward sign of the divine authority to which all, from Christ himself to the newest deacon, believed themselves servants.

Now as to the texts themselves. To begin with, though the evidence is limited and the occasions described somewhat diverse, there is the suggestion of a pattern to the rite of the laying on of hands which at least prefigures the later Christian tradition. Candidates for office are chosen and approved by the people, there is fasting and prayer, and then the laying on of hands with prayer, all of which passes directly into the liturgy of the ember days and the rites of ordination of the early Church and beyond.[7] There is also a consistency in these few texts in the theology of such commissioning. Candidates are selected because they recognizably already possess the Spirit (Stephen) or are pointed out to the congregation at prayer by the Spirit as being the most suitable (Barnabas and Paul). That is to say they already have gifts from the Spirit, equipping them to the task. At the same time the commissioning itself is regarded (at least in the Pastoral Epistles) as the act through which the candidate receives a gift (2 Tim. 1.6, 'rekindle the gift of God that is within you through the laying on of my hands'), the gift of course being from God in response to the prayers of the church.

But a number of questions remain. First, who commissions? In Acts 6, it is the apostles; in Acts 13, we don't know; in Acts 14, Paul, himself an apostle, together with Barnabas 'appoint' elders in every church, prays, fasts and commends them to the Lord. The word here is *cheirotonia* which technically means to elect by show of hands but which later is to become the normal term for ordination (e.g. in the Greek text of Hippolytus' *The Apostolic Traditions*). In the Pastorals, someone called Paul, who is an apostle, has laid hands on Timothy and Timothy in turn is warned to lay hands on no one suddenly, indicating that he also performs the rite (1 Tim. 5.22; cf. Titus 1.5). There is the question in 1 Tim. 4.14 of 'the council of elders' laying hands on Timothy. Some would quote this as evidence of appointment by a college of presbyters or see in it the origins of the modern 'rugby scrum' at a priest's ordination. But we have to be careful. 2 Tim. 1.6 clearly indicates that Timothy has been given the gift of God 'through the laying on of *my* (sc. Paul's) hands'. So too it is not the *elders/ presbyters* (plural) who are said to lay on hands in 1 Tim. 4.14, but the word used is genitive singular (*tou presbyteriou*), a collective term usually translated 'presbytery', and not genitive plural (i.e. 'of the presbyters'). D. Daube believes that the phrase 'when the council of elders laid their hands on you' is in fact a technical expression for the act of ordination, having nothing to do with presbyters actually laying on hands.[8] Whatever the case may be, Timothy undoubtedly has hands laid on him by Paul who is an apostle and the presbyteral participation is either a sharing in this or non-existent.

Second, who is ordained and to what office? The Seven in Acts 6 are commissioned for a particular work which could be described as diaconal, but they are never called deacons. In Acts 13, Saul and Barnabas are presumably among the 'prophets and teachers' and are simply sent 'for the work to which I have called them'. The fact that both are later called apostles cannot lead us to any hard-and-fast conclusion that this was the manner of appointing apostles who were not of the number of the twelve. (Matthias after all was elected, but that was to the original apostolic college.) Timothy, according to tradition, was the first Bishop of Ephesus, but there is nothing in the Pastoral Epistles to indicate this, though it is evident that he was appointed to a task of pastoral oversight and there is also an exhortation in the epistles on the office of a bishop, as there is an account of the qualities required of a deacon. Only in Acts 14 do we find Paul and Barnabas, both apostles, appointing presbyters in every church, though there is no reference here to the act of laying on of hands. The mention of prayer and fasting might however suggest that it was such a rite and relates to the account of Paul and Barnabas' own commissioning in Acts 13. So the real answer is that we do not know very much about the titles given to those commissioned by the laying on of hands. The tasks are various, the situations different. All that we do know is that by an early period this method of appointment to office was being used and had already a developing theology of the gifts of the Spirit.

It is equally difficult to ascertain from the New Testament evidence alone what form the ministry of those so appointed was to take. The work of the Seven in Acts 6 is briefly but clearly indicated; Paul and Barnabas are to be missionaries. Those appointed elders are also called bishops (Acts 20.28) and their task appears to be that of oversight and pastoral care for the new churches. At this period, there is no evidence of any single minister presiding over one Christian community; at Philippi there are 'bishops' (plural) and the word 'elder' rarely appears in the singular (as in 1 Pet. 5.1). Deacons, male and female, appear at intervals throughout the New Testament period (Phil. 1.1; Rom. 16.1), but we have no evidence that these were appointed by the laying on of hands. So what conclusions may be drawn?

First, though the rite we have been examining is used for the commissioning of a variety of ministries, it has nonetheless a central theme, namely the public acknowledgement of a person's suitability to perform the task designated and the declaration that through the outward sign of the imposition of hands and in response to the church's prayer, that person *has received a gift from God* by means of which he may now authoritatively undertake his new work (1 Tim. 4.14; 2 Tim. 1.6). The apostles themselves had been both commissioned (John 20.21, 'even so I send you') and received a gift (John 20.22, 'Receive the Holy Spirit') which was their warrant for their ministry (so far as the fourth evangelist is concerned). In all cases save one (about which there is uncertainty, viz. Acts 13) it is the apostles (or an apostle) who performs the rite of commissioning. A pattern seems to be emerging where-by certain offices in the Church, notably those of oversight and pastoral care, cannot be performed without such commissioning.[9]

Second, the titles given to what we shall now call the 'ordained minister' in the New Testament are basically descriptive of function or status and are not yet names for different grades of a hierarchy. It doesn't matter from the perspective of later generations that a bishop in the New Testament is not superior to a presbyter; nor does the fact that in the New Testament an elder can do the work of oversight and a bishop can belong to the number of the elders (Acts 20.28) mean that the church plunged into error in the early second century by exalting one above the other. The evidence suggests that in the foundation of new churches suitable men were appointed for the oversight of the community *and were considered equal in rank*. The diaconate apart, the apostles seem to have authorized *one ministry and one ministry only*.

Third, it matters little that some local churches in the New Testament period seem to have had a number of ordained ministers (bishops at Philippi and elders/presbyters at Miletus) whereas by the turn of the first century, many seem to have had only one. We are here in a developing situation and the emerging pattern of a Church for which one man is ultimately responsible does not make that Church a community that cowers to an auto-cratic despot, but emphasizes the role of that one man in the service of the unity of the local congregation.

Fourth, that the title 'bishop' finally emerged as the name given to the principal pastor of a local church is perhaps a sign of the depths of meaning in the term itself. In the Hebrew and Hellenistic world it simply means what it says – one who has oversight. But the real richness is discovered when Ezekiel (in the LXX text) writes about the shepherds (*episkopoi*) who have deserted the flock (Ezek. 34.1ff) and the fourth evangelist by contrast portrays Christ as the Good Shepherd who does not leave the flock (John 10.14); when St Peter in the same vein reassures the newly baptized that they were as sheep going astray but have now returned to the 'Shepherd and Guardian [bishop] of your souls' (*poimen kai episkopos*, 1 Pet. 2.25) and when St Paul warns the elders/presbyters of Miletus that they are to take care of 'all the flock, in which the Holy Spirit has made you overseers [bishops], to care for the church of God which he obtained with the blood of his own Son. I know that after my departure fierce wolves will come in among you, not sparing the flock' (Acts 20.28–29), a direct parallel with John 10. The leaders of the new Israel have to reverse the failures of the old, but they have for their example and strength the pattern and person of Christ the Good Shepherd, who has also given them the Holy Spirit.

Fifth and last, presbyters, when they appear again as different in rank to the bishop are not so much a new order as a derived ministry, or, one could say, an extension of the bishop's ministry. Ignatius of Antioch who tells us a little about this, is bishop of a large metropolis, the churches to which he writes are in sizeable towns. Already Christians are sufficiently numerous not to be able to meet in one place (house churches being too small and public buildings not at the Christians' disposal).[10] Hence presbyters ordained by the bishop, solely to assist the bishop (as Hippolytus indicates in the account of their ordination[11]), are able to do all that a bishop does except represent the whole local church (which is precisely why they do not share in the commissioning of new ministers). When the bishop is present, they always yield their presidency of the parish church to him; when he is absent, theirs is the *episcope* of the parish.

The ARCIC statement 'Ministry and Ordination' speaks of the origins of the ordained ministry as follows:

> The New Testament shows that ministerial office played an essential part in the life of the Church in the first century, and we believe that the provision of a ministry of this kind is part of God's design for his people. Normative principles governing the purpose and function of the ministry are already present in the New Testament documents (e.g. Mark 10.43–5; Acts 20.28; 1 Tim. 4.12–16; 1 Pet. 5.1–4). The early churches may well have had considerable diversity in the structure of pastoral ministry, though it is clear that some churches were headed by ministers who were called *episcopoi* and *presbyteroi*. While the first missionary churches were not a loose aggregation of autonomous communities, we have no evidence that 'bishops' and 'presbyters' were appointed everywhere ... Just as the formation of the canon of the New Testament was a process incomplete until the second half of the second century, so also the full emergence of the threefold ministry of bishop, presbyter,

and deacon required a longer period than the apostolic age. Thereafter this threefold structure became universal in the Church.[12]

This summary came under some criticism, and in the 'Elucidation', the authors replied:

Our treatment of the origins of the ordained ministry has been criticized. While the evidence leaves ground for differences of interpretation, it is enough for our purpose to recall that, from the beginning of the Christian Church, there existed *episcope* in the community, however its various responsibilities were distributed and described, and whatever the names given to those who exercise it ...[13]

This point is crucial. The name of the person or persons who either individually or jointly exercise *episcope* is immaterial. The important fact is that the Church in its structures should reflect the truth that oversight is a charge received and not solicited, is the exercise of authority in virtue of a prior obedience to a higher authority and as such is the complete reversal of the self-centredness of so many of the cheaper secular concepts of authority. The apostles are already warned that their sitting on thrones does not make them like the kings of the Gentiles (Luke 22.25–27). They have been chosen, often against their better judgement, they have been sent out not feeling themselves equipped for the task, they have been commissioned with a gift of the Spirit as the sole means of achieving anything in their mission. It is the rite of ordination, whose beginnings we have sought to trace, with its pattern of choice (John 15.16, 'You did not choose me ... I chose you'), commission (John 20.21) and gift (John 20.22) which is the outward and sacramental sign of the continuance of this structure of oversight and authority in the Church. 'From the beginning of the Christian church, there existed *episcope* in the community', no matter who exercised it. In itself it is an expression of Christ's continuing love and care for humanity; and today, after Christ the Good Shepherd, the Church calls her ministers bishops.

At the end of the first century AD, Clement, Bishop of Rome, writing to the Church of Corinth which was troubled by controversy concerning its ordained ministers, wrote:

Jesus Christ was sent from God. Christ then is from God, and the Apostles from Christ ... And so, as they [the apostles] preached in the country and in the towns, they appointed their first-fruits ... to be bishops and deacons of them that should believe ... Our Apostles knew also, through our Lord Jesus Christ, that there would be strife over the dignity of the bishop's office. For this reason therefore, having received complete foreknowledge, they appointed the aforesaid, and after a time made provision that on their death other approved men should succeed to their ministry ... (1 Clem. 42; 44)

This simple and direct statement from a witness who wrote within the period of the formation of the New Testament canon and who is quoted with reluctance by some because he is 'extra-canonical', may not be an accurate assessment of all the historical details but is a powerful testimony to what the early Church believed about commission, service, obedience and authority among the ordained ministry. For Clement, the true bishop is God himself ('Creator and bishop of every living soul', 1 Clem. 59), for St Peter who died at Rome, Christ is 'the Shepherd and Guardian (Bishop) of [our] souls' (1 Pet. 2.25). It is only this bishopric, conferred through the apostles to the ordained ministry by the gift of the Spirit, that can show the episcopate in the Church today to be both original and credible.

Excursus II – Episcopal Authority and the Ordination of Women

I have been rightly advised that a book on the subject of episcopal authority is in fact incomplete without some consideration of recent proposals in the Anglican Communion that women should now be ordained to the episcopate. The facts, briefly stated, are that over the past two decades, some provinces of the Anglican Communion have taken the decision to ordain women to the priesthood; and, secondly, that the experience of women in the parochial and non-parochial ministries, has in some places been so rewarding that it seems only logical and right that a woman, who for example has served for ten years as a parish priest, should be considered as a candidate for election and ordination to episcopal responsibility. Some opposed to the ordination of women look upon this proposed step as the ultimate blasphemy; on the other hand, those who support the movement sometimes wonder whether this should not have been mooted from the very beginning. The second order of ministry is after all a derived order, having its origins in the episcopate; and until women take their place firmly in the first order, then the Church will not have clearly said 'Yes' to the assertion that the ordained ministry of the Church at every level is for men and women alike.

This is obviously not the place to embark on a re-examination of the arguments for and against the ordination of women. In the Church of England, the debate is still in process and the General Synod has (at the time of writing) yet to propose to Parliament that the way forward for bishops to accept both men and women as candidates for ordination to the priesthood should be made legally and practically possible. However, two issues emerge in the debate which are closely related to the subject matter of this book.

The first is a very simple fact of everyday life in the Church of England. When the order of deaconess was revived in the nineteenth century, it was tacitly assumed that though they were ordained in the traditional manner, with prayer and the laying on of hands, deaconesses would live either in community (as many of them did, becoming more like a sisterhood than an extra task force) or as 'lady workers', attached to a parish. Legally, they were certainly not deacons. Being full time in the service of the church, they were invaluable as parish visitors, teachers, conductors of meetings and confirmation classes and pastoral counsellors (usually to the women of the parish). They had no liturgical function (other than that of conducting the divine office in community). Over the years, however, the office of deaconess has developed to such an extent that it is now very difficult, in some parishes, to distinguish between the work performed by a deaconess and that undertaken by a deacon or curate.

As well as the overall task of pastoral care which a deaconess will share with the parish priest, she is now expected to preach, assist with the distribution of Holy Communion, act liturgically as a deacon during the Eucharist, baptize, conduct funerals, prepare adults and children of both sexes for confirmation and in general to act as 'curate' to her vicar. In addition, the manpower situation in the Church of England is in some places so desperate, that a vicar may well leave the major pastoral responsibility of one of his parishes to a deaconess and simply appear when needed to celebrate the Eucharist, conduct marriages and give absolution. There are also parishes in the Church of England today where the bishop has judged it best to give the overall pastoral responsibility to a deaconess direct with the instruction that the local clergy are to provide a celebrant for the Eucharist when needed. In other words, some deaconesses today act either as full-time curate or 'priest-in-charge' of the parish.

It is here that the first major theological anomaly occurs. It has been argued in earlier chapters that the ministry of a presbyter or a parish priest is not an order invented to cope with the pastoral needs of parish life, but is essentially an extension of the episcopate. So much so that today, it is customary for the bishop when inducting or instituting a new incumbent to declare explicitly that the pastoral oversight of the parish concerned is 'Your care and mine', thereby making it perfectly clear that since he, the bishop, cannot possibly cope with all the churches, he appoints another to do his 'episcopal' work in each parish. Why should he not give such a charge to a deaconess provided that nearby clergy are willing to serve on a rota as Sunday celebrants of the Eucharist? But it is precisely here that the major difficulty arises. For the celebration of the Eucharist is the focal point of any ministry of pastoral oversight, not an additional item to parish life which can be performed by any suitably qualified and commissioned clergyman. The bishop cannot therefore appoint a deaconess and tell her that she is to gather the people of God around her and bind them into a unity as a worshipping and serving body when at the very moment the people of God assemble in church as a body corporate for worship, she, their pastoral leader and guide, has to step down while a relatively little-known clergyman takes over at the altar. The pain felt by many deaconesses in such a position is understandable. For if a deaconess is to be given charge of a parish, logically she should before taking up her duties, be given authority to act as the bishop's deputy; in other words she should be ordained priest. Similarly, if a deaconess is asked to act as a curate and to share the vicar's overall pastoral responsibility, it is she who should act as the vicar's deputy in his absence. It is logically absurd, for example while the vicar is on holiday, for a deaconess to conduct the Eucharist up to and including the intercessions and then to 'hand over' to a visiting priest for the absolution (after the general confession) and the eucharistic prayer. Presiding at the Eucharist (which presumably includes the liturgy of the Word) is again the task of the bishop's deputy – not simply that of someone competent to read, lead the prayers and to preach. In other words, once more, a deaconess asked to perform a liturgical and pastoral ministry of this kind should very clearly be ordained priest.

The above, however, must not be taken as the author's conviction that the time has now come to ordain women to the priesthood. It is simply an appeal to the Church of England to sort out a fairly substantial theological nonsense. We need either to say that the ministry of a deaconess is that of a unique kind of pastoral assistant in a parish, an order in the Church (and there is no cause whatever to consign deaconesses to the ranks of the laity) which is not that of *deputy* to the parish priest but has its own functions, privileges and duties. Or we have to say that the deaconess is in her ordination like a deacon and (since we have no theology of the perpetual diaconate) must act as a curate, and therefore needs (either immediately or eventually) the same authority as a curate expects to receive, namely ordination to the priesthood. It is current pastoral need (among other things) that has led the Church of England to emphasize this latter role. It must now

either go forward to resolve the anomaly and agree to the ordination of women to the priesthood or it must decide more precisely
what the role of a deaconess is today within the structures of the
Church's ministry and cease giving to women responsibilities with
one hand and witholding authority to carry them out with the
other.

The first theological consideration must therefore be that if the
bishop of a diocese wishes to give pastoral responsibility to a man
or woman either in full (as to an incumbent) or as deputy (as to a
curate) – on the understanding that the deputy may on occasions
assume full responsibility – then the only order to which he can
ordain is that historically known as the presbyterate, and today
generally called the priesthood. If he (and the church which he
represents) is opposed to this arrangement, then he must make it
perfectly clear that in ordaining to the order of deaconess, he is
intending to continue an ancient and clerical order which has
certain clearly defined functions within the Christian community
(and which may have liturgical expression) but which are not
those of pastoral oversight such as is exercised by the parochial
priesthood and its immediate assistants (in deacon's or priest's
orders).

The second issue is perhaps more serious. A variety of reasons
is given today for not admitting women to the order of priesthood.
God, it is said, became incarnate in the person of the *man*, Christ
Jesus; Christ's chosen apostles were exclusively male; two thou-
sand years of the apostolic ministry has known only men ordained
as bishop or priest. The celebrant of the Eucharist, representing
as he does in words and actions Christ's own 'parable' of his
passion and resurrection at the Last Supper, needs therefore to be
an image or 'ikon' of that same essentially male figure of the
Redeemer.

Opposed to this, it is argued that God, though represented in
Scripture as male, is himself the source of all masculinity and
femininity; that his incarnation as *man* fitted a particular context
of history and theological expectation when only a male Messiah
would have fulfilled the Jewish hope and made the concept of
'God coming in the end' credible; that feminine language is not
only applied to (or implied in) talk about God, but is also used
occasionally of Jesus (Julian of Norwich calls Jesus 'our Mother')
and of the Holy Spirit (who has a feminine title in Gnostic and

early Syriac pneumatology); that the subordinate place given to
women in the Church of the apostolic age was due mainly to the
social conventions of Roman, Greek and Jewish society; and that
the current reappraisal of the proper role of women in society
today suggests that a ministry, long forbidden to women by the
Church's male-dominated hierarchy, should now be confidently
opened to all, with women taking a leading part as bishops and
priests.

This is a debate that has generated a good deal of heat – and,
psychologists will not have been slow to note, more than a measure
of the irrational – on the part of traditionalists and progressives
alike. It is not, moreover, a debate that is likely to be concluded on
the basis of one set of arguments clearly outweighing another.
The decision – for or against – when it comes, will be a community decision and in this country will be made by the General
Synod, with a majority (probably fairly small) having failed to
convince the rest of the rightness of whatever course of action is
resolved upon.

It is here that the Church of England should stop once more
and consider the implications of such a procedure. To begin with,
there is no theological justification for the Church of England to
take such a decision entirely on its own initiative. The Church of
England consists of two provinces of a relatively small communion
of churches; that communion, however, is a reality. Though historically it developed from a group of colonial and missionary
churches (all heavily dependent upon their country of origin) into
a loose federation of autonomous provinces, it has become in our
own time very much more conscious of its unity and of the mutual
interdependence of the member churches.

Though individual provinces have exercised a legitimate freedom in deciding independently to make the ordination of women
part of their regular ministerial policy, without feeling the obli-
gation to seek the general approval of the whole communion, over
the past decade there has developed what can perhaps be described as a 'centrifugal movement' among Anglicans, suggesting
that mutual consultation and the seeking of agreement in matters
of doctrine and discipline ought to be a prime characteristic of a
worldwide communion of churches, and not an option to be
considered or rejected by each province as it chooses. It is precisely this new climate (ably encouraged by the present Archbishop

of Canterbury and by the Anglican Consultative Council) which should make the Church of England aware that a vote in the General Synod, involving all the inevitable political infighting of contemporary ecclesiastical parties, is probably not the right way to reach a decision about the ordination of women to the priesthood in this country.

The initiative of the recent meeting of Anglican Primates in requesting a working party to examine the issue of the appointment of women as bishops is in this light a very important recommendation. For members of any province of the Anglican Communion, the sense that a major decision such as this lies not within the power of a relatively small synod of powerfully motivated delegates, but rests rather with a worldwide union of Church leaders (many of whom are fully conversant with administering dioceses where women already serve in the priesthood) is a tremendous reassurance. It has already been made clear in earlier chapters that a synodical gathering of bishops is both the traditional and probably the most effective way of assessing the mind of the whole Church and of making firm proposals for consideration and reconsideration. That being so, the Lambeth Conference of 1988 could well serve the entire communion on this very sensitive issue in a reassuring and effective manner.

It must also be remembered that Anglicans are not simply in communion with one another but share a fellowship with other episcopal churches. The 'wider episcopal fellowship', as it is known, is normally – and in the most limited sense – taken to include other churches possessing an episcopal ministry in the apostolic succession with whom Anglicans have the right to share communion at the same altar, and whose members are similarly received in all churches of the Anglican Communion. But this is a very narrow interpretation of what is described as 'full communion'. When Old Catholic bishops, for example, come to take part in the consecration of Anglican bishops, this is not to confer 'validity' (in the eyes of Roman Catholics for example) lest Anglican ordinations should be still held doubtful by the Roman and Orthodox communions, but the act of an Old Catholic bishop's laying on of hands is a declaration that the church which he represents is in full communion and fellowship with the church which the new bishop now represents and with all other churches of the Anglican Communion.

If this is so, then it is small wonder that the Old Catholic churches of the Union of Utrecht took exception to the unilateral decision of the American Episcopal Church to ordain women to the priesthood without prior full consultation. At the time, there was an equally unfortunate decision on the part of the Polish National Church in America to break communion with American Episcopalians. This was deplored by the then Archbishop of Utrecht who declared that schism was not the answer to serious disagreements and that the matter should be resolved within the communion of churches. But, again at the same time, a statement by an Anglican Old Catholic Conference which met at Chichester in April 1977 declared that since there was 'no consensus between the churches on either the theology or discipline involved in the ordination of women to the priesthood ... before any future decisions are taken on matters of importance which affect the relationship between our Churches, more effective organs of consultation than we have at present should be established and used'. Here again the Anglican Communion had an opportunity to demonstrate its membership of and dependence upon the widest possible Christian fellowship; it should certainly bear this in mind today. It should also perhaps be added that the Old Catholic churches are by no means a 'brake' on the movement to ordain women to the priesthood. There is widespread opinion among some of their theologians that such a step is in fact appropriate, but that full agreement between all the churches involved should be reached before the final decision is taken.

But what finally of the two great communions of the Orthodox East and of the Roman Catholic Church? It is no exaggeration to say that Orthodoxy is frankly amazed that the Anglican Communion should even consider such a step, a judgement which was perhaps predictable and seen by many to lie in the Orthodox insistence that the priest at the altar stands very much as the 'ikon' or in the *persona* of Christ and therefore must be incontrovertibly male. But, once again, this is to see their objection in the narrowest light. One shock reaction from the United States by an Orthodox theologian included the observation that not only was the American Episcopalian action in ordaining women to the priesthood theologically indefensible, but that to decide upon such a move 'by vote in the General Synod' was almost the worse blasphemy. We forget all too often that the

Orthodox churches are probably more emphatic on the need for episcopal synodical gatherings than any other communion in Christendom. For this, the elected synods of the Anglican Communion are no substitute. Rather, the only way, in the Orthodox view, to discern the mind of the Church under the guidance of the Holy Spirit is to assemble the churches in the person of their bishops and to seek the mind of Christ by prayer, fasting and concentrated theological debate. Hence their disquiet about Anglican proceedings is as profound about method as it is about content and deserves serious Anglican attention.

Similarly, the warning sounds coming from the Roman Communion in recent months about the serious obstacles to reunion raised by the movement within Anglicanism to make the ordination of women as priests a regular feature of Church life, need to be considered in the light of more than just the usual run of arguments for and against such a policy. That two Roman Catholic priests recently signed an open letter to the Bishop of London in favour of the ordination of women may well indicate that there is more than a nominal groundswell within Roman Catholicism as a whole to support Anglican practice in some provinces. But this is not the real issue. When Anglicans and Roman Catholics have spent the greater part of seven years in compiling a joint agreed statement, *Authority in the Church*, in which it is explicitly declared that it is the role of the bishops in collegiality with one another to discern the mind of the whole Church on major questions of belief and practice, for a small group of bishops with their elected synods in a single province to arrogate such decisions to themselves without full consultation seems a contradiction of all that has been claimed to have been achieved after years of a growing together in painful but fruitful association. What the Roman Church seems to be saying is: 'If we are going to work together, let us begin now. By all means bring your new insights, your new proposals with you. But please show that you are in earnest and that you wish to share these with us; so that when a decision is made, even if it is to allow women to exercise the priesthood in certain places, under certain circumstances, this is the decision of us all and will enrich us all.'

The Church of England today is in a unique position. On the eve of making perhaps the most important decision so far about the ordination of women to the priesthood, it has the chance to say that whatever is decided by the General Synod this year must be referred in the first instance to the whole Anglican Communion in order that the communion as a whole, with all the insights that it has to offer, may assess and then recommend what might be a suitable policy for any or all of the Anglican provinces.

It would be very sad if the Church of England were to be looked upon as 'the last bastion to fall' as a grudging vote in its General Synod initiated the long legal proceedings to remove all barriers to the admission of women to all levels of the ordained ministry. Much better would be the sense that the Anglican Communion as a whole had, after reflection upon existing experience, decided that it had something unique to contribute to Christendom by showing that both men and women could effectively serve together in the one apostolic ministry of bishop, priest and deacon.

But the Anglican Communion has other commitments. First, as we have shown, to the wider episcopal fellowship, and in this to the Old Catholic churches in particular. The Old Catholics of the Union of Utrecht have been more than generous in standing firm to the Bonn Agreement of 1931 which declared a state of 'full communion' on the basis of agreement on 'all the essentials of the faith'. It is understandable that some anxiety has been caused by the unilateral decision of the American Episcopalian Church (for example) to ordain women to the priesthood. Old Catholics look not only to the Roman Communion (to which perhaps they are closest) but also have strong relationships with the Orthodox, and they do not wish relationships in either of these directions to be compromised by the fact that they remain in communion with Anglicans who are pursuing a policy in the ordination of women which is strongly opposed in official circles by both Rome and Constantinople. They admit that there is no consensus of opinion among themselves and Anglicans on the matter; but they have requested full consultation which must mean that should the Anglican Communion go ahead with a regular practice of ordaining women to the priesthood, then the Old Catholics should accept this as a feature of 'legitimate diversity' in the Church as a whole (always remembering that some of their own people would like to see such a diversity among the churches of the Union of Utrecht!). It is to be hoped, therefore, that any working party set up by the Anglican primates to discuss the admission of women to the episcopate would at some stage involve theologians and bishops from the wider episcopal fellowship in its consultations.

But perhaps most important of all, if the Church of England is prepared to concede that the way forward to reunion with Rome and the Orthodox involves the rediscovery of the collegiality of the bishops of all churches, then the opening up of episcopal consultation (as has been proposed in chapter 6) with an issue such as the ordination of women high on the current agenda is probably paramount. Here once more it is conceivable that a midway solution might be that the Roman and Orthodox churches might see the Anglican experience of women in the priesthood as an exploration (much as the Roman Church today is beginning to admit in some circumstances, albeit exceptional, the possibility of a married priesthood) and accept it as a phenomenon in a very diverse landscape.

However, what both Rome and the Orthodox understandably cannot appreciate is a communion of churches which reaches out to them in friendship, asking for unity and practical cooperation, but which continues to treat as a private and internal matter an issue which is of concern to the whole of Christendom. If there is to be any progress, any relaxation of tension over this issue, any rediscovery of the full scope and potential of Christian ministry to the modern world, then the honesty and openness with one another of the bishops of all communions is the essential prerequisite. And it may well be that the Anglican Communion will have to be the first to acknowledge the need for a regular interchurch episcopal conference.

The way of ecumenism is the way of the cross. This does not necessarily refer to the pain and difficulty that is felt by any who have seriously laid to heart the sheer senselessness that divides them from those they are naturally disposed to love and respect at the deepest level of life's wonder and mystery. The way of the cross is the way of self-denial, not of self-despising or self-hatred, but involving a willingness to abandon a world in which everything seems right and ordered and harmonious to the ear, for a world in which the self is muted and listening. Like a brilliant solo musician who suddenly finds himself a member of a string quartet, there are entirely new skills to be learned, new delicacies to be appreciated, new balances to be maintained, an entirely new experience to be drowned in, and baptized to a new resurrection. Only such a disposition among the bishops of all churches can forward their understanding of one another and of the Spirit's leading onwards to the Church of the future.

Notes

Chapter 1

1. G. K. A. Bell, *Randall Davidson* I (Oxford 1935), p. 569.
2. ibid., p. 301.
3. Church of England Archbishops' Commission, *Church and State: The Report of the Archbishops' Commission* (London 1970), p. 15.
4. C. Morris, *Political Thought in England from Tyndale to Hooker* (Oxford 1953), p. 192.
5. Appendix to Church of England Assembly (Powers) Act, 1919, cit. Cripps, *Law Relating to the Church and Clergy* (London 1920), p. 28.
6. ibid., p. 26.
7. Bell, *Randall Davidson* I, p. 149.
8. Report of the Royal Commission on Ecclesiastical Discipline (1906), para. 5, cit. Bell, *Randall Davidson* I, p. 473.
9. cf. A. Vidler, *The Church in an Age of Revolution* (Harmondsworth 1961), p. 127.
10. Report, Church of England Archbishops' Commission, *Government by Synod* abridged version (London 1966), p. 3.
11. General Synod Constitution, para 7.

Chapter 2

1. Richard Hooker, *Laws of Ecclesiastical Polity* II. viii. 7 in John Keble (ed.) *Works* I (Oxford 1888), p. 336.
2. Peter Gunning, *The Paschal or Lent Feast*, Library of Anglo-Catholic Theology (Oxford 1845), p. 18.
3. William Beveridge, *Sermon LI*, in *Theological Works* II (Oxford 1851), p. 435.
4. Robert Boyle, *Works* II (London 1772), p. 260.
5. Daniel Whitby, *An Answer to Sure Footing* (Oxford 1666), p. 28.
6. M. Luther, *An Appeal to the Christian Nobility*, cit. H. Bettenson, *Documents of the Christian Church* (Oxford 1963), p. 195.
7. cf. Gordon Rupp, *Luther's Progress to the Diet of Worms* (London 1951), p. 38.
8. On Calvin's theology of the ministry, see K. D. Mackenzie in K. Kirk (ed.), *The Apostolic Ministry* (London 1946), pp. 469ff.
9. *Anglican–Methodist Unity. II – The Scheme* (London 1968), p. 182.

10. M. Wiles, *The Remaking of Christian Doctrine* (London 1974), p. 48.
11. H. B. Green, *The Gospel According to Matthew* (Oxford 1975), p. 251.
12. Interestingly, Archbishop Theodore at the Synod of Hertford (673) allows a man to leave his wife on grounds of the Gospel exception, but not to marry again if he wants to be a 'good Christian'.
13. Anglican–Roman Catholic International Commission, *The Final Report* (London 1981), pp. 52–67.
14. ARCIC, *Final Report*, p. 52.
15. G. H. Tavard, *Holy Writ or Holy Church* (London 1959), pp. 202, 207–8.
16. ibid., pp. 195ff.

Chapter 3

1. Bede, *A History of the English Church and People* (Harmondsworth 1968), IV.5.
2. See A. H. Thompson, *The Cathedral Churches of England* (London 1925) for an admirable account of the English dioceses after the Conquest.
3. On the bishop during this period, see J. R. H. Moorman, *Church Life in England in the Thirteenth Century* (Cambridge 1945) and W. W. Capes, *A History of the English Church in the Fourteenth and Fifteenth Centuries* (London 1903), pp. 218ff.
4. In the *Dogmatic Constitution on the Church* (*Lumen Gentium*) in A. Flannery (ed.), *Vatican Council II – The Conciliar and Post Conciliar Documents* (Dublin 1975), pp. 350ff.
5. *Lumen Gentium* 26 cit. Flannery, *Vatican II*, p. 381.
6. G. Baum, *The Constitution on the Church of Vatican Council II* (London 1964), p. 21.
7. N. Afanasieff in *Ecclesia a spiritu sancto edocta* (Louvain 1972), p. 215.
8. Emmanuel Lanne, 'The Local Church, its Catholicity and Apostolicity' in *One in Christ* (London 1970–3), p. 312.
9. On episcopal elections in antiquity see J. Bingham, *Antiquities of the Christian Church* (London 1856), IV, 1 and 2.
10. cf. Clement of Rome, *Letter to the Corinthians*, 42 and 44.
11. Irenaeus, *Adversus Haereses* III.iii.1ff.
12. Optatus, *On the Schism of the Donatists* II.iv.41ff.
13. Gregory Nazianzen, *Theological Oration* 21.8.
14. Augustine, *Sermo* 146.1.1.; *Ep.* 217; *Sermo* 49.2.
15. See the Excursus 'The Origins of the Episcopate', pp. 76ff.
16. Described in R. Krautheimer, *Early Christian Architecture* (Harmondsworth 1965), ch. 1.
17. Hippolytus, *Apostolic Tradition* 8.1.

18. Joseph Bingham, *Antiquities of the Christian Church* II.12ff.
19. Cyprian, *Epistola ad presbyteros et diaconos* 5.4.
20. Capes, *A History of the English Church in the Fourteenth and Fifteenth Centuries*, pp. 240–2.
21. cf. A. E. Harvey, 'Attending to Scripture' in Doctrine Commission of the Church of England, *Believing in the Church* (London 1981), pp. 25ff.
22. See Y. Congar, *Jalons pour une Théologie du Laicat* (Paris 1953), passim.
23. H. Küng, *Structures of the Church* (London 1965), pp. 67ff.
24. These principles are set out in R. W. Dale, *A Manual of Congregational Principles* (London 1894).
25. C. Morris, *Political Thought*, p. 118.
25. B. J. Kidd, *A History of the Christian Church to AD 461* 3 (Oxford 1922), p. 202.
27. Bell, *Randall Davidson* II, p. 1353.

Chapter 4

1. Text in Harduin, *Acta Conciliorum* I (Paris 1715), cols. 247–58.
2. See Küng, *Structures of the Church*, pp. 64ff.
3. 'The Holy Spirit and Inspiration' in C. Gore (ed.), *Lux Mundi* (London 1890), p. 360.
4. Letter 105 to his brother in J. Stevenson (ed.), *Creeds, Councils and Controversies* (London 1966), pp. 264–7.
5. G. S. R. Boase in *Dictionary of National Biography* (Oxford 1894), pp. 264–6.
6. Bell, *Randall Davidson* I, pp. 292–3.
7. Account in Kidd, *History of the Church to AD 461*, pp. 403–6.
8. E. J. Yarnold and H. Chadwick, *Truth and Authority* (London 1977), pp. 16–17.
9. Kidd, *History of the Church to AD 461* II, pp. 403 and III, pp. 162.
10. Yarnold and Chadwick, *Truth and Authority*, p. 18.
11. P. I. Bratsiolis, 'The Fundamental Principles and Main Characteristics of the Orthodox Church' in A. J. Phillipou (ed.) *The Orthodox Ethos* (Oxford 1964), p. 30.
12. On the Church at the time of the Conquest see Thompson, *Cathedral Churches*; on the fifteenth-century Church see Capes, *A History of the English Church in the Fourteenth and Fifteenth Centuries*.
13. On Convocations at the time of the Reformation, see T. Lathbury, *A History of the Convocations of the Church of England*. London 1842.
14. cit. W. H. Frere, *History of the English Church and People – The Reigns of Elizabeth and James I* (London 1904), p. 91.

15. *The Second Note of the Church examined*, cit. P. E. More and F. L. Cross, *Anglicanism* (London 1957), p. 141.
16. W. H. Hutton, *A History of the English Church and People from the Accession of Charles I to the Death of Anne* (London 1903), pp. 278ff.
17. cit. F. W. Cornish, *A History of the English Church and People – The Nineteenth Century* Part I (London 1910), p. 333.
18. Bratsiolis, 'Fundamental Principles'.
19. ARCIC, *The Final Report*, p. 54. cf. *The Alternative Service Book* (London 1980), p. 388, order for the ordination of a bishop, in which the bishop's duties are declared to include not only the guardianship of the faith but also the interpreting of the gospel of Christ.
20. Ignatius of Antioch, *Letter to the Trallians* 1.1.

Chapter 5

1. Text in G. K. A. Bell, *Documents on Christian Unity* 1920–1930 (Oxford 1955), pp. 156–69.
2. Listed in N. Ehrenstrom and G. Gassmann, *Confessions in Dialogue*. Geneva 1975.
3. Groupe des Dombes, *Pour une Réconciliation des Ministères*. Taize 1973.
4. cf. General Synod 300, *Visible Unity in Life and Mission* (London 1976).
5. Churches Council for Covenanting, *Towards Visible Unity: Proposals for a Covenant* (London 1980).
6. cf. the *Memorandum on the Status of the Existing Free Church Ministries*, 1924 in Bell, *Documents on Christian Unity*, pp. 156–63.
7. *Towards Visible Unity*, p. 22.
8. ibid., p. 17.
9. For an account of Methodist senior ministers see *Anglican–Methodist Unity – II. The Scheme* (London 1968), pp. 40–2.
10. *Towards Visible Unity*, pp. 29–31.
11. ibid., p. 15: 'Within this Covenant we undertake to respect the rights of conscience and to accord to all our members such freedom of thought and action as we jointly agree to be consistent with the visible unity of the Church. Will you respect these rights and maintain this freedom?'
12. ibid., p. 15: 'Within this Covenant we bind ourselves to develop methods of decision-making in common, to act together for witness and service, to aid one another in Christian growth and to honour the authority of shared decisions.'
13. *Anglican–Methodist Unity – I. The Ordinal* contains both a statement of common belief about ministry in the preface and a rite of ordination. London 1968.

14. The term 'character' is not used here in the technical Roman Catholic sense of ordination conferring 'character' appropriate to the order being bestowed.
15. Groupe des Dombes, *'Pour une Réconciliation des Ministères*, p. 30: 'En raison de la situation crée par la rupture du XVIe siècle, nous reconnaissons que nous sommes privés non de la succession apostolique, mais de la plénitude du signe de cette succession.' (On account of the situation brought about by the sixteenth-century schism, we acknowledge that it is not the apostolic succession that we lack, but the fullness of the sign of this succession.)
16. *Anglican–Methodist Unity – I. The Ordinal*, preface, para. 6.
17. C. O. Buchanan, *Growing into Unity* (London 1970), p. 122.

Chapter 6

1. ARCIC, *The Final Report*.
2. ibid., p. 99.
3. ibid., p. 67.
4. *Towards Visible Unity*.
5. *ARCIC, The Final Report*, p. 44.
6. cf. R. A. Noel, *The Church of England – Is Reunion Possible?* (London 1961), p. 8.
7. See H. Brandreth, *Episcopi Vagantes and the Anglican Church*. London 1947.
8. cf. ARCIC, *The Final Report*, pp. 36–7.
9. This view is implicit in B. C. Butler's *The Idea of the Church* (London 1962), in which he questions the possibility of those who separate from unity being considered 'churches'. Schism, he considers, is always 'from the church'; to talk of 'schism in the church' is a contradiction in terms. But see his *The Church and Unity*. London 1980.
10. St Irenaeus of Lyons, *Adv. Haer.* III.3.1.
11. G. G. Willis, *St Augustine and the Donatist Controversy* (London 1950), gives a full and vivid account of the course of the schism.
12. ibid., pp. 153, 154 for texts illustrating this.
13. *Lumen Gentium* 1.8.
14. The *Decree on Ecumenism* 13, however, states: 'The Anglican Communion has a special place among those which continue to retain, in part, Catholic traditions and structure.'
15. Translated and annotated by M. Bévenot in *Ancient Christian Writers* 25, London 1957.
16. The essence of Cyprian's teaching is to be found in chapters 4 and 5 of the *De Ecclesiae Catholicae Unitate* (London 1957), Bévenot's notes are important.

17. *Episcopatus unus est cuius pars ab omnibus in solidum tenetur*, Cyprian, *De Ecclesiae* 4.
18. I have argued this elsewhere in R. J. Halliburton, 'St Cyprian's Doctrine of the Church' in F. L. Cross (ed.) *Studia Patristica* (Berlin 1972), pp. 193ff.
19. op. cit., p. 57.
20. Ignatius of Antioch, *Letter to the Smyrneans* 8.
21. cf. J. Danielou, '*Mia ekklesia* dans les Pères Grecs des Premiers Siècles' in *L'Église et les Églises* (Paris 1965), p. 138. 'L'Église unique c'est l'Église antique, celle qui existe depuis les origines et non pas celle qui existérait seulement au terme ... L'Église n'est pas le résultat mais la cause de l'union des chrétiens.'('The one Church is the original Church, the one that has existed from the very beginning and not the one that would exist only at the end ... The Church is not the result but rather the cause of Christians coming together.')
22. cf. E. J. Yarnold, *Anglican Orders, A Way Forward?* (London 1977), p. 14, who emphasizes that the Anglican Communion is considered in the Decree on Ecumenism to have preserved in part Catholic *structure* (italics his).
23. cf. ARCIC, *The Final Report*, pp. 81ff for a consideration of these issues.

Excursus I

1. Ignatius of Antioch, *Letter to the Trallians* II.1. and III.1.
2. ibid., loc. cit.
3. Ignatius of Antioch, *Letter to the Smyrneans* 8.1.
4. The Reformation reaction is described in K. D. Mackenzie, 'Sidelights from the Non-Episcopal Communions' in Kirk, *The Apostolic Ministry*, pp. 461ff.
5. On Old Testament and Rabbinic parallels, see E. Lohse, *Die Ordination im Spätjudentum und im Neuen Testament* (Göttingen 1951) and J. Coppens, *L'imposition des Mains et les Rites Connexes* (Paris 1925). See also D. Daube, *The New Testament and Rabbinic Judaism*. Oxford 1955.
6. Though the term becomes the normal Greek equivalent of *ordinatio* by the beginning of the third century, as in Hippolytus' *The Apostolic Traditions*.
7. Described in Bruno Kleinheyer, *Die Priesterweihe im Römischen Ritus* (Trier 1964), pp. 35ff.
8. Daube, *New Testament and Rabbinic Judaism*, pp. 224–6.
9. cf. *I Clement* ch. 44, written *c.* AD 95.
10. R. Krautheimer, *Early Christian Architecture* (Harmondsworth 1965), ch. 1.
11. Hippolytus, *Apostolic Tradition* 8.1.
12. ARCIC, *The Final Report*, p. 32.
13. ibid., pp. 42–3.

Bibliography

Chapter 1

Bell, G. K. A., *Randall Davidson*. 2 vols. Oxford 1935.
Cripps, S., *Law Relating to the Church and Clergy*. London 1920.
Kemp, E. W., *Counsel and Consent*. London 1961.
Lathbury, T., *A History of the Convocations of the Church of England (to 1742)*. London 1842.
Lloyd, R., *The Church of England in the Twentieth Century*. London 1926.
Morris, C., *Political Thought in England from Tyndale to Hooker*. Oxford 1953.
Vidler, A., *The Church in an Age of Revolution: 1789 to the Present Day*. Harmondsworth 1961.
Weske, D. B., *Convocation of the Clergy*. London 1937.
Reports: Church of England Archbishops' Commission, *Government by Synod*. London 1966.
Church and State: The Report of the Archbishops' Commission. London 1970.

Chapter 2

Congar, Y., *La Tradition et les Traditions*. Paris 1960 (ET *The Tradition and the Traditions*. London 1966.)
Cullmann, O., *La Tradition*. Paris 1953.
Dodd, C. H., *The Authority of the Bible*. London 1929, revised 1960.
Herbert, A. G., *Fundamentalism and the Church of God*. London 1957.
Moran, G., *Scripture and Tradition*. London 1973.
More, P. E., and Cross, F. L., *Anglicanism* (London 1957), pp. 89ff.
Tavard, G. H., *Holy Writ or Holy Church*. London 1959.
Taylor, V., *The Formation of the Gospel Tradition*. London 1933.
Thornton, M., *The Function of Theology* (London 1968), ch. 1.

Chapter 3

Baum, G., *The Constitution on the Church of Vatican II*. London 1964.
Congar, Y., *Jalons pour une Théologie du Laicat*. Paris 1953. (ET *Lay People in the Church*. London 1957.)
Capes, W. W., *A History of the English Church in the Fourteenth and Fifteenth Centuries*. London 1903.

The Authority of a Bishop

Küng, H., *Structures of the Church*. London 1965.
Moorman, J. R. H., *Church Life in England in the Thirteenth Century*. Cambridge 1945.
Morris, C., *Political Thought in England from Tyndale to Hooker*. Oxford 1953.
Telfer, W., *The Office of a Bishop*. London 1962.
Thompson, A. H., *The Cathedral Churches of England*. London 1925.
Reports: *One in Christ*, 3. 1970.
 ARCIC, *The Final Report* (London 1981), pp. 30–45.

Chapter 4

Frere, W. H., *A History of the English Church and People*. (Other volumes by W. H. Hutton, London 1903, and F. W. Cornish, London 1910.)
Küng, H., *Structures of the Church*. London 1965.
Lathbury, T., *A History of the Convocations of the Church of England*. London 1842.
Moore, P., *The Synod of Westminster: Do We Need It?* London 1986
Phillipou, A., *The Orthodox Ethos*. Oxford 1964.
Yarnold, E. J. and Chadwick H., *Truth and Authority*. London 1977.

Chapter 5

Buchanan, C. O. *et al.*, *Growing into Union*. London 1970.
Reports: Anglican–Methodist Unity Commission, *Anglican–Methodist Unity: I. The Ordinal, II. The Scheme*. London 1968.
 Churches Council for Covenanting, *Towards Visible Unity: Proposals for a Covenant*. London 1980.
 Groupe des Dombes, *Pour une Reconciliation des Ministères*. Taize 1973.
 General Synod 300, Visible Unity in Life and Mission. London 1976.
 General Synod 307, *The Reconciliation of Ministries*. London 1976.

Chapter 6

ARCIC, *The Final Report*. London 1981.
Butler, B. C., *The Idea of the Church*. London 1962.
idem, *The Church and Unity*. London 1980.
Cyprian of Carthage, *On the Lapsed and on the Unity of the Catholic Church*, (translated and annotated by M. Bévenot). Ancient Christian Writers XXV. Maryland and London 1957.
Greenslade, S. L., *Schism in the Early Church*. London 1964.
Willis, G. G., *St Augustine and the Donatist Controversy*. London 1950.

Index